£1

Speaking for Myself

SIR ROBIN DAY's television career began in 1955. After war service in the Royal Artillery, he read Law at Oxford University. In 1950 he was President of the Oxford Union. He was called to the Bar in 1952 and practised briefly. In 1955 he became one of ITN's original newscasters. In 1959 Sir Robin joined BBC *Panorama*, to which he contributed for 30 years. He presented Radio 4's *The World at One* from 1979 to 1987. He chaired *Question Time* on BBC TV for ten years from 1979.

Awards for his work have included the Richard Dimbleby Award in 1975, and the Royal Television Society Judges' Award in 1985. Sir Robin was knighted in 1981. He is an Honorary Bencher of the Middle Temple.

His memoirs, *Grand Inquisitor,* were a best-seller on publication in 1989. He has two sons and lives in London, where he was born in 1923.

SPEAKING FOR MYSELF

Sir Robin Day

EBURY PRESS

By the same author

Television: a Personal Report (1961)
The Case for Televising Parliament (1963)
Day by Day: a Dose of My Own Hemlock (1975)
Grand Inquisitor, memoirs (1989)
...But With Respect: memorable TV interviews (1993)

First published in Great Britain in 1999

1 3 5 7 9 10 8 6 4 2

Ebury Press
Random House · 20 Vauxhall Bridge Road · London SW1V 2SA

Random House Australia Pty Limited
20 Alfred Street · Milsons Point · Sydney · New South Wales 2061 · Australia

Random House New Zealand Limited
18 Poland Road · Glenfield, Auckland 10 · New Zealand

Random House South Africa (Pty) Limited
Endulini · 5A Jubilee Road · Parktown 2193 · South Africa

www.randomhouse.co.uk

Random House UK Limited Reg. No. 954009

Papers used by Ebury Press are natural, recyclable products made from wood grown in sustainable forests.

A CIP catalogue record for this book is available from the British Library.

ISBN 0 09 186796 7

Printed and bound in Great Britain

To my splendid sons
Alexander and Daniel

CONTENTS

INTRODUCTION

I n this collection of speeches, the reader is offered more entertainment than education, more wit than wisdom, more amusement than argument. They were speeches for special occasions, festive and solemn. They celebrate, congratulate, or commemorate, with malice toward none, with charity for all.

Some were delivered to well-wined audiences in the banqueting halls of grand hotels. Others were in conferences, seminars, literary lunches and literary launches, university debates and award ceremonies. Some were in church for memorial services. Several were at famous functions, such as the Colchester Oyster Feast, or at glittering gatherings like the Variety Club of Great Britain, the Saints and Sinners, the Grand Order of Water Rats, or the Lord's Taverners. And of course those anniversary banquets beloved of the BBC.

Toasts are proposed. Anecdotes are told. Legs are pulled. Insults are harmlessly hurled. Jokes are cracked — even on the more solemn occasions. Compliments are paid, not without humour and mischief, to old friends and great contemporaries — a colourful assortment of celebrities, including Morecambe and Wise, Ted Heath, Roy Jenkins, Margaret Thatcher, Geoffrey Howe, John Cole, Harold Wilson, Paul Fox, Paddy Mayhew, Ludovic Kennedy, Moira Shearer, Chris Chataway, Ronald Waterhouse, Milton Shulman, Geoffrey Cox and Sue MacGregor. For Aidan Crawley, Robert Carvel and Ivan Yates, three great friends and mentors, there are *éloges* — affectionate tributes given at their memorial services. And in a speech about Winston Churchill, the dramatic story is told of the events, hour by hour, of May 10th, 1940, the day when he became Prime Minister, to the dismay of the Tory establishment.

There are three "lectures" (to use an off-putting word). One was to doctors about my multiple heart bypass operation. Another was to Bar students about the law of libel. A third was to lawyers about why our courts should not be televised.

This miscellany is not presented as oratory, or literature, or comedy. It includes some "after-dinner" speaking, but there is also *before*-dinner speaking and after-*lunch* speaking. Audiences have varied from the near drunk and disorderly to the stone-cold sober.

These are speeches in one man's style and one man's sense of humour. All were a mixture of both the lovingly polished and the hazardously impromptu. Sometimes I was the sole speaker. On other occasions my speech was one of several on the oratorical menu. This did not matter if I happened to be less dreary than the others. But it could mean an uphill struggle, as when I rose to address the Grand Order of Water Rats at approaching midnight. Or at the famous Colchester Oyster Feast, when I was the last of seven speakers after a Lucullan lunch.

Ever since my schooldays, I have been interested in the art of speech-making. I even hoped for a career in a speech-making profession – as a barrister, or as a Member of Parliament perhaps. I did not get very far with either of those aspirations. I lacked the first-class brain to be a first-class barrister, and I have never been driven by overweening political ambition. But I have always continued to make speeches, not by way of advocacy or argument, but when invited, on special occasions.

The hypercritical reader may note that one or two phrases are used more than once. I am somewhat embarrassed to see "with even more than my usual humility" in almost every speech. My other regulars include "I have reached the departure lounge of life" and "I, alas, am not one of those broadcasters who have brought happiness into your hearts or merriment into your homes".

Rightly or wrongly, I have not edited all these out. Experience shows that a self-deprecatory, mildly humorous line can come in handy when the going is hard. What public speaker or performer (politician, comedian, headmaster, barrister or whatever) has not drawn on a stock of tried and trusted one-liners, if only as ice-breakers or defrosters? Anyway, the casual reader, who dips into this collection and does not read through every one, may not notice, or may not be too irritated by repetition. At least I hope so.

But I do plead guilty to having included in this collection, not

once but several times, a particular story about a certain eminent
and Right Honourable gentleman. In mitigation I can only plead
that the story is an old favourite of mine, going back 30 years. I
love telling it. Audiences love hearing it. It has never failed to
bring the house down. And the eminent and Right Honourable
gentleman, at whose expense the story is told, has forgiven me
every time he has heard it.

Perhaps I should have included it only once in this collection.
But I asked myself this: when is a story or line a favourite and a
classic, and when is it stale and hackneyed? After all, would we
want "a handbag" to be cut from *The Importance of Being Ernest*
merely because it has delighted audiences again and again, every
time the play has been performed? To those who find that
argument specious, I can only beg forgiveness.

The pleasure I have got out of speech-making has not been
that of performing, or of hearing my own voice, but the infinitely
more satisfying pleasure of making people laugh. There is no
sound more gratifying, indeed thrilling, than that of several
hundred people laughing happily, especially if they have not
expected to be amused at all.

I have never aspired to be a professional stand-up comedian.
But even when speaking on a sad or serious occasion, I have
sought to weave a strand of gentle humour into the fabric.

The reader will find here no stirring oratory, no impassioned
advocacy, no bitter hostility. No causes are championed. No
sermons are preached. No reputations are demolished.

These speeches should be read by ear. They are printed as
spoken,[1] not as literary essays. It is difficult, if not impossible, to
convey in print the subtleties in tone and expression and timing
of speech. Even so, someone who browses with imagination
through this miscellany may sense the spirit and style of the
original as it was delivered.

In some cases, the texts have been transcribed from a sound or
television recording. Mostly they have been typed up from the
notes used by me at the time – notes which were revised if

---

[1]Hence the printing in lines of irregular length may look almost like blank verse! Because I,
like others, have long been addicted to the Churchillian 'psalm form' of script. See Speech 23,
pages 132–3.

necessary to include ad-libbed changes or additions. The only editing has been to minimise repetition and to remove the superfluous, the obscure and the incomprehensible.

These are the speeches of an amateur, not of a professional. To introduce each one, I have written a brief scene-setting note to explain where, when and why it came to be made.

Only one speech in this collection was made for a fee. That was my address to a professional symposium of cardiologists and other doctors about my multiple heart bypass operation. My Scottish hosts offered a fee, which I accepted. Otherwise what is it, you may ask, that has made all this speech-making worth my while? "Nothing," in the words of Hilaire Belloc, "but laughter and the love of friends."

Robin Day
London, 1999

M ay 13th, 1967 at the Hampstead home of Sir Geoffrey Cox, CBE. Few invitations to speak have delighted me more than that from Sir Geoffrey and Lady Cox to propose the health of their twin daughters, Evelyn and Rosamond, on their 21st birthday.

I had served at ITN under Sir Geoffrey's distinguished Editorship for three exciting years, 1956–59. I am greatly in his debt for the wise advice and opportunities he gave me. When I left ITN in 1959 for BBC *Panorama*, we remained firm friends. I met him and his family at home and on holidays. In 1967, their teenage twins had grown into glamorous undergraduates and were 21.

Since then, both have achieved marriage, motherhood, and professional distinction. Rosamond is now a consultant microbiologist in the National Health Service. Evelyn became a journalist, has written two highly acclaimed books, and has been a farmer. She now runs a large bookshop in Hay-on-Wye.

The occasion gave me an opportunity not only to toast the talented twins, but also to indulge in a little respectful badinage at their father's expense.

Lady Cox, Sir Geoffrey, Ladies and Gentlemen:

It is, of course, a pleasure and an honour
to propose a toast to Rosamond and Evelyn this evening.
Nothing else really needs to be said.
And I want to make it clear that it is only through affection
for Sir Geoffrey and Lady Cox and for their daughters
that I have been able to conquer
my natural aversion to making any kind of speech.

You will appreciate the delicacy of my task.
Not even the Director-General of the BBC,
let alone the Editor of ITN,

has faced a more difficult problem of balance
and impartiality than I face tonight.

On such a delightful occasion as this,
it is hardly a problem which can be solved in my usual fashion –
by being equally offensive to both parties.

So what can I say of Evelyn and Rosamond,
who look so lovely here tonight –
covered with the modesty and diffidence of contemporary youth –
as they happily anticipate the gross flattery
which I shall heap upon them?

We must not only congratulate them,
but congratulate their father and mother
on reviving in such fine style
a charming notion of a bygone age,
the nostalgic idea that coming-of-age
does not occur until the 21st birthday.
A courageous reaction against the prevailing spirit
of the times in which we live.

For in an age when infants exhibit
their paintings in the Royal Academy,
and teenagers are the supreme trend-setters of national life,
21 is surely the very brink of retirement.

So I rejoice to be present at this elegant
and dignified celebration held so defiantly
in the heart of swinging Hampstead.

I have not known Rosamond and Evelyn
for *all* of their 21 years.
But I've known them for about half that time.
Any suggestion that I was probably fortunate
not to have met them before the age of 11
is unworthy of this happy occasion.

My first recollection is of them
with their hair in beautiful plaits
which were approximately the same length
as the skirts they now wear in Bristol and Oxford.

My knowledge of them indeed goes back a long way,
back to those far-off days when their father feared
that their morals would be corrupted
by watching commercial television.

Every time I have met them over the last ten years
they have been taller, prettier and cleverer.

As an ex-employee of their distinguished father,
I am bound to say that their many fine qualities
come almost entirely from their mother.
But as a possible *future* employee of their father,
I must hasten to point out
that they have inherited from him
at least one powerful gift, that of self-projection.

Rosamond's photograph was on the front cover of *Cherwell*
almost before she had unpacked her books at St Anne's.
Not to be outdone, Evelyn posed glamorously in Bristol
for the *Daily Express* in connection with some incident
whose details are not wholly clear to me.

Rosamond and Evelyn have always resisted
what I can only call "the twin image".
The natural contrast of their personalities
has been given full expression.

They have been to different universities,
studied different subjects, acquired different interests,
and there is every reason to believe
that they will marry different husbands.

They are, in fact, determined individualists.
Rosamond is almost the only medical student nowadays
who does not want to be a psychiatrist.
And in her more serious activities on the magazine *Cherwell*,
she has revealed such a talent for writing
that one wonders how long she will practise medicine.
Will she perhaps add a feminine name
to that celebrated list of doctor-authors
which spring so easily to mind –
A J Cronin, Richard Gordon, Somerset Maugham

and Lord Hill of Luton –
And what name is more hallowed in this house?[1]

Evelyn's studies of economics and politics have not,
I'm happy to say, interfered too much
with her responsibilities as propaganda chief
of the Bristol Students' Union,
where I am told she has manipulated
the mass media to great effect.

She will soon be working on the business side
of *The Economist* where she'll be able to acquire
that business acumen which her father may come to envy
as he surveys his own record
of helping other people to amass their fortunes.
The only really gainful deal Sir Geoffrey has ever pulled off
was when his wife gave him two daughters for the price of one.

So as Rosamond and Evelyn approach
the end of their crowded university careers
we wish them brilliant success in their final examinations.
Their university lives seem to have been so crowded
that I am reminded of a contemporary of mine
whose tutor sent him a newspaper advertisement
which said, "Why not spend your leisure time reading for a degree?"

Ladies and Gentlemen, we are commemorating a memorable event.
Although the 21st birthday of Rosamond and Evelyn
was actually on Thursday, I think today
can be taken as the anniversary. For May 11th, 1946 was a Saturday.
It was very considerate of Rosamond and Evelyn to make their appearance
on a day when Parliament was not sitting.
Their father, Political Correspondent of the *News Chronicle*,
was thus free to concentrate on the major event at Westminster that week –
the birth of his twin daughters in Westminster Hospital.

Otherwise, May 11th, 1946 was another day
in the drab, austere life of post-war Britain.
On that Saturday 21 years ago,

[1] Lord Hill, formerly the Radio Doctor, was then Chairman of the Independent Broadcasting
Authority, under whose aegis came ITN and Sir Geoffrey.

London was getting its first coat of paint for the Victory Parade.
The Political Correspondent of the *News Chronicle*
had only a brief item running in his four-page newspaper,
about a promising Labour back-bencher, Mr Hugh Gaitskell,
who had been given his first Government post.
The cheese ration was about to be reduced
from three ounces to two ounces per person per week.

And the long-suffering populace kept their spirits up
by whistling the top tune of the month,
which, in May 1946, was "Money is the Root of All Evil".
A sentiment, I hasten to say, not shared
by the Political Correspondent of the *News Chronicle*.

I wonder if Rosamond and Evelyn realise the problems
their joint arrival caused in those austere times.
Their father was then a humble working reporter,
not yet glittering with rank or title.
When his joy was tempered by realising
that there would now be two extra mouths to feed,
he very nearly made the supreme sacrifice.
He thought of going back to work for Lord Beaverbrook.

That, then, was the setting for the event we celebrate tonight.
To Rosamond and Evelyn we wish happiness, romance and long life.
I will not reveal any of their romantic secrets,
except to say that in the current national fashion
they appear to have kept their options open.
As to long life, they will certainly have that
if they take after Sir Geoffrey's father,
whom I visited in New Zealand five years ago
when he was over 90 years of age.
Not only was he full of vigour,
but at half-past three on a warm New Zealand afternoon
he said, with a guilty twinkle in his eye,
"If you'd have a glass of whisky,
I should have to join you."

And if your glasses are now full, I give you the toast,
Rosamond and Evelyn.

2 QUALES ARTIFICES PERIMUS

D ecember 7th, 1967 at the Oxford Union, for the first time in 12 years. This was the "Farewell" Debate of Robert Jackson, President in the Michaelmas term of that year. Traditionally, the last debate of term is a light-hearted affair on a motion which means very little. The motion was in Latin: "*Quales artifices perimus*".

At that time I was very busy with my work on BBC *Panorama*. I did not want the trouble of preparing the kind of speech required on a nonsense motion. I remembered from my undergraduate days that making a good speech on a meaningless motion was infinitely harder than making a good speech on, say, the crime wave or the Common Market.

But I agreed to speak, because the 21-year-old President was an undergraduate at my old college, St Edmund Hall.

Robert Jackson was formidably clever. He went on to achieve a brilliant academic record, taking a First in History and becoming a Fellow of All Souls. In 1983 he was elected a Conservative Member of Parliament, and in 1987 he was appointed a junior minister in Mrs Thatcher's administration.

Despite the pretentious Latin motion, I was fortunately able to make the most of an unprecedented event. This was the recent election of Miss Geraldine Jones (St Hugh's College) as the first woman President of the Oxford Union. In congratulating her, I forecast a brilliant future for her in public life. I could not have been more wrong. She has not been heard of since. According to the latest Union history, she married, and became Mrs Greineder, in Germany. Probably her life has been happier than if she had become an MP or a television personality. Anyway, she seemed to relish her fleeting few weeks in the limelight at Oxford.

In the end I enjoyed myself at the brainy Mr Jackson's Farewell Debate. He took my mockery with great good humour.

Mr President, Sir:

It gives me great pleasure to add my support
to the motion "*Quales artifices perimus*".

It would give me even greater pleasure
if I knew what the hell it was about.

It is a long time since I sat in your chair
at the turn of the half-century.
Seventeen years ago, in fact, when you, Sir, were a babe in arms,
a white imperialist brat on the Rhodesian copper-belt,
and I was giving the final flourish
to the golden age of post-war Oxford.

I must confess surprise at the levity of this debate so far.
It is certainly not what I expected.
Who would have imagined
that for an evening intended to be humorous
the two visiting speakers would be from *Panorama* and *Punch*?

But it is always a pleasure to be back in Oxford.
For those who work in the materialistic community outside,
it is exhilarating to breathe
the pure air of the academic world,
where all are dedicated to the selfless pursuit
of truth and excellence.

But Oxford, of course, is not beyond reproach.
Can its reputation ever recover
from having produced all three leaders
of our present political parties?
Two of them, indeed, from this very Society
and from the chair which you, Sir, occupy.

It was here that Mr Edward Heath decided
that he was better at political leadership
than at playing the organ.
It was here that Mr Jeremy Thorpe saw himself
as the man to whom the nation would turn
sooner or later.

Mr Harold Wilson, however, did not frequent this hall.
Shrewd as ever, he busied himself elsewhere,
acquiring his mastery of economics.
Not only that. Here in this university
was born Mr Wilson's famous pragmatism.
Having won the Gladstone Memorial Prize,
he spent the money
on the collected works of Disraeli.

Mr President, Sir, this is the first time
that I have spoken in this Society since it became bisexual.
I recall the fierce arguments against the admission of women –
that the President would too easily succumb
to the wiles of unscrupulous young women.
Or that Presidents would use their position
to debauch innocent creatures
who had thrown themselves at their feet.

It was also suggested (would you believe it, Sir?)
that women were less rational than men.
That women would spoil the languid, elegant style
which you, Mr President, embody
with almost imperceptible effort.

The worst argument was that women would use sex
to undermine the whole basis of the Society's elections.
That luscious young women would hang around the premises
like fruit ripe to be plucked,
ready to surrender their virtue for our votes.

I realised that argument was somewhat overdone
when I heard that 698 votes were cast for the President-elect.[1]
Surely merit played some part in *her* overwhelming victory?

Allow me to offer her my sincere congratulations
on being elected as your successor.

[1] Miss Geraldine Jones (St Hugh's College), the first woman to be elected President of the Oxford Union.

She has achieved a First — more glittering than any First
which an examiner will ever award her —
which is no doubt a considerable relief.
She is inescapably labelled for life.
Whatever she does — her successes, her failures,
her marriages, her divorces —
will all inevitably be coupled
with her achievement here.
No news editor will ever forget her.
She has an eternal identity tag
in the files of Fleet Street.
Her private life has gone for ever. From now on,
she will live in the relentless spotlight of publicity.
But whatever her future, whether she moves on
to great achievement or, like me,
she ends up on television,
she will surely rank
among the immortals of this Society.

Must we wait for 50 years for her to have
a place of her own along these walls?
I am delighted to hear, Mr President,
that you are setting up an expert committee
of ex-Presidents to arrange
for the unveiling of her bust.

However hard I try, I cannot escape the motion
which I am proposing.
When you notified me of its terms,
I was somewhat puzzled.
I telephoned the Society. I asked for the President.
I had to wait some time.
I understand you had a couple of long-distance calls
to eminent personages about their coming visits here —
the Pope and Mao Tse Tung, I believe you said.

Eventually your elegant voice came on.
I said, hoping to conceal
my confusion about the Latin motion,
"What translation are you using?"
You replied, "Robert Graves has done rather a good one."
I said, "Not bad at all."

You went on helpfully,
"It's just a little thing from Suetonius."
"Of course," I said, recalling
that at the BBC Television Centre
scarcely an hour passes without our enjoying
a few quiet moments with our well-thumbed copies of Suetonius.

"Do you think anyone will turn up?" I asked.
"Oh yes," you replied. "Mr Basil Boothroyd of *Punch*
will be a very big draw."

Greatly encouraged, I began to study the motion more carefully.
The more I did so, the more depressed I became.
Several anxious questions began to shape in my mind.
Why should I be saddled
with the dying words of the Emperor Nero? [1]
Was Nero the kind of man
with whom my name should be linked?
What did these words really mean?

Research confirmed my hazy recollection
that Nero was a thoroughly disreputable young man
with extremely nasty habits.
These habits included –
and I will not go into more detail than the House wishes –
incest, rape, castration, indecent assault and exhibitionism.
Nero was, in fact, a notable pioneer of the permissive society.
He murdered practically all his relatives,
including several of his wives, his mother
(who was also his mistress) and his aunt.
His aunt, I notice, was an elderly lady
who was constipated at the time.
Nero murdered her by administering what is described
as "a laxative of fatal strength".

Yet this is the man with whom my name
and my likeness are linked on your defamatory order paper.
As the ex-President from Wadham, Mr F E Smith,

[1] Nero's last words, as quoted in Suetonius' *Lives of the Caesars*, were, "*Quales artifices perimus!*"
(sometimes translated as, "What an artist dies with me!").

said in that famous five-word, 1,000 guinea opinion,
"The damages should be enormous."

So in moving this motion,
I wholly dissociate myself from the Emperor Nero.
I will not go into any further details
of this man's disgusting life.
But for Honourable Members
who wish to pursue their own researches,
I thoroughly recommend this rare edition
of a very old translation of Suetonius' *Twelve Caesars*.
This, Mr President, is the sought-after 1606 translation.
Much more vivid and authentic
than the bland euphemisms of Robert Graves.
Merely by having it in my hand, I risk prosecution.

But if I hold no brief for Nero,
how can I possibly support the motion?
The answer is that one must ignore
the literal meaning of those words, whatever it may be.

What the motion really means is this:
that Robert Jackson has been a great and brilliant President
and the sole object of this occasion
is that this House begs him to accept,
albeit reluctantly, their humble admiration.

That being the real meaning,
I was not prepared to support it without investigation.
A number of people have helped me with my enquiries,
with no motive against you except sheer malice.

You have been summarised as a "colonial
who has managed to acquire polish".
Politically, you appear to be loosely Liberal
with a Marxist past and a Tory future.
You have shrewdly avoided the embarrassment
of any party allegiance, or the crudity
of having any firm political convictions.
You are skilfully poised
to have a political career in any convenient direction.

But I understand that your aspirations
are less political than academic –
that you intend to become a don.
As Nero would have said,
de gustibus non est disputandum.

Mr President, your brief moment of glory is almost over.
You have tasted power as you may never taste it again.
By all reports it has suited your palate perfectly.

I have no hesitation in supporting this congratulatory motion,
Quales artifices perimus.
Or, as a much nobler Roman said,
Sic transit gloria Edmundi.[1]

~

---

[1] The minimal adaptation of the ancient Latin "*sic transit gloria mundi*" was by way of a convenient reference to "*Aula Sancti Edmundi*" (St Edmund Hall), the college where President Robert Jackson was then an undergraduate.

BBC's 50th ANNIVERSARY 3

February 6th, 1973, Dorchester Hotel. The BBC's Golden Jubilee had been in November 1972 and was celebrated with prolonged enthusiasm. There were so many special events that this luncheon for the BBC's 50th Anniversary, given by the Variety Club of Great Britain, had to be delayed by a few months until 1973.

The Chief Barker – Eric Morley (of "Miss World" fame) – presided, and proposed a toast to the BBC. The BBC's Director-General, Sir Charles Curran, responded. I seconded the Director-General's response.

Mike Yarwood, the brilliant impersonator of politicians and lesser folk like myself, was then at the height of his popularity.

Lord Hill of Luton, the ex-Tory Cabinet Minister, had just retired as Chairman of the BBC. He had earlier made his name as the Radio Doctor who talked about constipation at breakfast-time on the BBC. The new BBC Chairman was Sir Michael Swann, FRS.

Mr Chief Barker:

As this is a serious occasion
it is only fair to point out to the audience
that you labour under a misunderstanding:

My name is Mike Yarwood. Of course, if you want me
to do my well-worn impersonation of Robin Day
I will. But I would much rather not.
Because I have done it so often
that I now suffer from one of his nightmares,
in which he begins an interview
with a leading politician as follows:
"What is your answer to my first question?"

But if you insist, I will do as you bid,

though my enthusiasm is tempered
by the painful recollection of what happened last time
I followed Mr Eric Morley,
which was immediately after his "Miss World" contest.
During the two seconds it took for the announcer to say,
"And next on BBC 1,"
I lost the BBC 15 million viewers.
There has been nothing like it
since the flight of the Gadarene Swine –
or the collapse of the Conservative vote
in the Sutton and Cheam by-election.[1]

It is a happy thought that the Variety Club of Great Britain
has invited not only the boss,
but me, one of the lowly workers of the BBC.
I am a mere cog in the great machine.
So in the presence of so many masters from upstairs,
I speak from downstairs with even more than my usual humility.

Not least among the Director-General's heavy burdens,
is the responsibility he bears for every word I utter –
on screen and at the microphone.
But he has no responsibility
for what I am about to say here.
All I can suggest is that the Director-General
should now take a stiff drink and hope for the best.

In addition to being the executive head and editor-in-chief,
the Director-General is an impresario
who presides over the greatest collection of variety acts,
the richest feast of performing arts,
that the world has ever seen.
From Alf Garnett to Civilisation.
From Michael Parkinson to Monty Python.
From Morecambe and Wise to Heath and Wilson.
From the sublime to the … Right Honourable.

As I look around at this galaxy
of popular entertainers and personalities,

---

[1] Two months earlier the Liberals had easily won in a blue-chip Tory seat.

I realise how ill-fitted I am for this happy occasion.
Alas, I am not one of those broadcasters
who bring gladness into your hearts
or laughter into your homes.

I am sometimes forced to wonder
whether I am a human being.
Because during my years in television
I have often been upset by continually being likened
to various members of the animal kingdom.
In the press and in viewers' letters I have been described
as a grizzly bear, a wolfhound, a terrier, a bull, a badger and a pig.
And a rattlesnake is how Miss Jean Rook described me.
But now you know why the Prime Minister chose
as the new BBC Chairman an eminent zoologist.[1]

Last November, the 50th anniversary celebrations of the BBC
were rightly full of nostalgia and pride in the past.
Though one visitor was confused –
the American you may have heard of,
who was under the impression that the Queen
was celebrating her Golden Wedding to Lord Reith.

Today we can look forward.
The first half of our century is behind us.
A new era of broadcasting has begun.
A new Chairman has been appointed.
We all extend to him our good wishes – and good luck.
The BBC, one might say, is over the Hill.[2]

What extraordinary explosions of controversy
can be sparked off by that little grey box!
Blank screens! Granada's World out of Action!
Programmes banned and unbanned.
Injunctions imposed one week, lifted another.
Learned judges gravely divided
on complex questions of constitutional law.

[1] Sir Michael Swann, FRS, Vice-Chancellor of Edinburgh University, later Lord Swann.

[2] Lord Hill had retired from the BBC Chairmanship.

And always somewhere – like the sad lady
in Keats's immortal od – Mrs Mary Whitehouse
standing in tears amid the alien porn.
The problem of sex on television raises difficult questions.
In this, as in all matters of morality,
the BBC will keep a balance.
There is no truth in reports that extracts
from Mr Marlon Brando's new film *Last Tango in Paris*
will be shown in the next edition of *Come Dancing*.

If the day ever comes when nobody criticises the BBC,
it will be because the BBC is not worth criticising.
It is preferable that the criticism should bear some relation to fact,
and I do not invite you to swell
the contents of the Director-General's mailbag.

But criticism should not be resented, but welcomed
and heeded as a measure of the high standards
which people have come to expect from their BBC.
And those standards can be summed up
in three words: integrity, excellence and fairness.

I gladly second the Director-General's response to this toast.
I do so on behalf of all those broadcasters
who in the last 50 years have built up those standards,
and of those who will try to uphold them
in the second half of this century.

Mr Chief Barker, thank you.

D ecember 10th, 1973, the Café Royal. The Lord's Taverners, whose name originates in the Tavern at Lord's cricket ground, are another of those convivial organisations whose members include many stars of show business and sportsmen, which raise funds for charity. Prince Philip is the Patron and the Twelfth Man.

In their own words, the *raison d'être* of the Lord's Taverners' fund-raising is "to give the young, whether disabled or not, a sporting chance".

At the Lord's Taverners' Christmas Lunch in 1973, my task was, in the bleak mid-winter, to propose the toast of Cricket. A recording of that speech was televised during the subsequent summer when rain had stopped play somewhere.

Mr President, Lord's Taverners:

There is, I see, bewilderment
on many of your faces as to why on earth
I should have been invited to propose
the toast of Cricket at the Lord's Taverners' Christmas Lunch.

Mr President, I have been a lover of the game since boyhood.
As a boy of ten, behind the pavilion
of the Wagon Works ground in Gloucester,
I obtained the autograph of the great Wally Hammond.
A few years later, in 1938,
I was present at the Oval
when Len Hutton made his mammoth record score,
which you will recall, Mr President,
was 364 caught Hassett bowled O'Reilly.

That was the historic occasion which I associate
with the greatest of cricket broadcasters,
whose recent death saddened us all, Howard Marshall.
Who can forget his memorable and classic line

delivered in that warm, rich voice,
discussing a slow, majestic game of cricket
on a glorious summer day in pre-war England:

> Hutton has been in 12¼ hours.
> England's total is 707 for 5,
> and the gasometer is sinking lower and
> lower.

My own playing of cricket
was undistinguished though enthusiastic.
When, as a small boy, I was given a cricket bat,
I insisted on taking it to bed with me
for many months. If any psychiatrists are present,
they should not draw any hasty conclusions.
In due course I transferred my attachment
to other objects of affection.

As a schoolboy, I was never more
than a modest "change" bowler,
and was changed very frequently.
As an undergraduate, my principal sport was
what many of you will recognise as the antithesis of cricket
– namely politics. I did quite well at it.

As President of the Oxford Union
I got a blue for waffling.

But I watch and follow cricket
with considerable zest.
I have even less connection with the world of show business –
of which so many Lord's Taverners
are glittering representatives –
than with cricket.
I am, alas, not one of those broadcasters
who bring laughter into your homes,
gaiety into your hearts.
I am a herald of gloom and conflict.

I have, however, had my moments
in the world of entertainment.

I have appeared as a guest on the television show
of two famous Taverners, Morecambe and Wise.
I felt that appearing with them would add
a new dimension to my television image,
and would launch me on a new phase of my career.
And it did.
I was offered work in the religious period on Sunday evening.
Morecambe and Wise, by the way, are currently appearing at the
    Hippodrome, Scunthorpe,
in a Christmas pantomime called *The Importance of Being Ernest*.

May I now explain
why we should drink a toast to Cricket:

First, it's another excuse to refill your glasses.

Second, this is what my speech is supposed to be about.

Third (here I come, you will be pleased to know,
to the climax of my remarks),
cricket is the supreme achievement of British civilisation.
Yes, greater even than the BBC
or our beloved trade union movement.

Why is cricket our supreme achievement?
What about the other wonderful things
we have given to an ungrateful world?
British justice, parliamentary government?

But, Mr President, where would British justice
and parliamentary government be without the values
of cricket to inspire and uplift them?

Only the other day, Lord Chancellor Hailsham himself
(speaking in a wholly non-political capacity
at the Junior Carlton Club)
was proclaiming the British tradition
of constitutionality –
which, he said, we are apt to call by homelier names –
"fair play, sportsmanship, decency and *cricket*".
All this, Lord Hailsham declared, is at the heart

of the British way of life
and, if it were lost, the rule of law
would fly out of the window.

So by supporting and encouraging cricket,
the Lord's Taverners are not merely supporting
and encouraging a game.
You are preventing the rule of law
from flying out of the window,
and Lord Hailsham from flying off the handle.

In the art of cricket we can see all those qualities
of the good life which the modern world is losing –
style, grace, elegance, tranquillity, patience.
And that quality which mystifies all foreigners,
the subtle excitement which is felt
on a summer's afternoon, when the sound of ball
against bat awakens one
from deep and alcoholic slumber.

Lovers of cricket cannot be complacent
at this critical time in the life of the country.
Dangers and difficulties lie ahead.
You must be prepared for change.
A cricket pitch will soon have a new length.
Not 22 yards but 20.1 metres.
The effect of this change could well be incalculable.
In the Tavern itself the pint will give way to the litre.
Since a litre equals just over 1¾ pints,
Taverners will learn to absorb
such a change with fortitude.

You will be sorry that time does not permit me to give,
my views as a cricket-lover on inflation,
industrial unrest and the energy crisis.
Suffice it to say that cricketers see
clouds gathering and skies darkening.
In fact, an appeal against the light
will soon be in order.

But in this prevailing gloom we should give thanks
to the Great Umpire for one small mercy:
at least we are not dependent on the Arabs for linseed oil.

Mr President, I ask you all, Taverners and guests,
to drink the toast to the immortal game, Cricket.

5 AN UNLIKELY HUMORIST

Mo ay 14th, 1974, Dorchester Hotel. The Variety Club of Great Britain was holding one of its famous lunches, to honour Eric Morecambe and Ernie Wise. The audience included entertainers, comedians and celebrities of stage, screen and radio.

I had made friends with Eric and Ernie when I had appeared on their television show. I was flattered that these two brilliant entertainers, then at the peak of their popularity, should have asked me to speak in their honour in front of so many stars of show business.

There were six guest speakers. We were each instructed to speak for not more than three minutes. They were André Previn, Glenda Jackson, Robert Morley, Francis Matthews, Graham Hill and myself. I, of course, kept to my three minutes, which came to six with laughter. I was quite nervous about it, until I heard the other guest speakers.

1974 being the year of two general elections, politics were much in the air. Also in the topical background was some scandal, and the need to "disclose an interest".

This Variety Club lunch was shown on television. Hence there were press notices. Mine were almost too flattering.

According to the *Western Morning News*, "An unlikely humorist emerged at the Variety Club celebration for Morecambe and Wise in Robin Day."

Under a heavy-type headline "Robin Day Stole the Show", the *Glasgow Sunday Post* reported, "Biggest surprise of the week? Viewers say it was Robin Day's comedy turn at the Morecambe and Wise Lunch."

But what pleased this "unlikely humorist" most was that his "comedy turn" was reprinted verbatim by these master comedians in their 1974 book *The Best of Morecambe and Wise*.

Mr Chief Barker, Ladies and Gentlemen:

I have a feeling that this occasion
is not really up my street.
Here are all these glittering stars
of the entertainment world, and here am I,
a messenger of gloom and conflict.

It is first of all my painful duty
to declare a financial interest.
Some years ago I was offered a sum of money
if I would agree to appear
on *The Morecambe and Wise Show.*
Believe me, at the time
I had every reason to believe
that they were absolutely respectable people.

My motives were entirely innocent. I simply wanted
to add a new dimension to my professional image.
I wanted to bring laughter into your hearts
and happiness into your homes.
But I wasn't even allowed to smile.
All the scriptwriter's genius was spent on my *only* line,
which was, "Good evening.
With me now are two leading politicians."
Eddie Braben must have sweated blood over that one.
And then do you know what happened?
Morecambe and Wise just hogged the whole thing.

But seriously: why is it that they
have inveigled me on to their show?
Why is it that I am invited here today
to join in the gross flattery of these proceedings?
The fact is that Morecambe and Wise
are not quite as simple as they look.
Do not be deceived by their happy
and contented faces. Because (I have to say this)
they are bitter and frustrated men,
whose supreme ambition has hitherto eluded them.

How can that possibly be?

Have they not done extremely well, considering?
Have they not won nearly as many awards
as Glenda Jackson?

Oh yes! They have indeed gone a long way
since that historic night, 33 years ago,
when together they shook the Empire
to its foundations. No madam,
I am talking about the *Liverpool* Empire.

In spite of it all they are still good friends –
nothing more. They have quarrelled only once
and that was when Mr Morecambe strongly objected
to taking part in Mr Wise's well-known play
The Importance of Being Ernest.

Their comic genius has even been psychoanalysed
and interpreted for us by Mr Kenneth Tynan
in the *Observer.* Yet they are still popular.
So famous have they become that the greatest actors
and actresses of stage and screen
jostle for invitations to appear on their show.
Miss Vanessa Redgrave invited them to
join her Workers' Revolutionary Party.
But their Rolls-Royces ran out of petrol on the way.

So what possible ambition can they have left?
I will tell you. It is to appear
in the most sensational television occasion of all,
the all-night spectacular – which for them
means the "Big Time", and which they have never achieved –
the general election night results programme.[1]
That is their secret dream. *That* is why I am here today.
That is what they long for:
Ernie on swingometer and Eric on computer.

But now they realise there is only one way
to achieve that ambition.

---

[1] 1974 was the year of two general elections. There had been one in February 1974 and another was
expected. It came in October 1974.

They are going to stand for Parliament
at the next general election
so that they can be candidates who will appear on TV.
They are looking now for suitable constituencies.
The most suitable they have found so far
are two neighbouring constituencies,
Old-ham East and Old-ham West.
And think what Eddie Braben
would have charged for that one.

Ladies and Gentlemen: it has been a very great pleasure
to attend this memorial serv… this tribute luncheon.
At the end of their show, Eric and Ernie
always sing their song "Bring me Sunshine".
It is *they* who bring *us* the sunshine
and may they continue to do so for many years.

IVAN YATES, 1926–1975

February 27th, 1975, St Bride's, Fleet Street. This was at a thanksgiving service for Ivan Yates, one of my closest friends. He had been killed, aged only 48, in a road accident. He was a much respected political journalist on the *Observer*.

The presence of his aged mother, so stricken with grief, made me dread the duty of saying what had to be said. But just before the service, Mrs Yates came over to me and said, "Don't forget Ivan had a sense of humour, will you?" That request was a great relief to me. I knew that she would not want a depressing tribute, devoid of any comic reminiscence.

St Bride's was packed with Ivan's fellow-journalists and parliamentary friends. They included Roy Jenkins, Bernard Levin, Harold Lever, Jeremy Thorpe, Lord Goodman and (from the *Observer*) David Astor, Anthony Sampson and Michael Davie.

As I was walking out of the church after my address, Roy Jenkins, that connoisseur of speech-making, kindly took me aside to compliment me on my address. "In fact," he added, "I thought it was almost perfect."

That coming immediately after an address which had been a strain to deliver came as comforting relief. Yet a few moments later I began to be riddled with doubt. "*Almost*" perfect? What exactly did the master mean? What had I, in error, included or omitted? Was there some minuscule defect of style? My dear old friend Ivan would have derived much humour from the nagging self-doubt which hit me after receiving a compliment which was really most generous.

Ivan's mother has asked me if I would speak about him
on this occasion, which is so very sad for us all.
Though you will notice that this is happily
not called a *memorial* service, but a service of thanksgiving
for the life and work of Ivan Yates.

His mother is with us here today.
Mrs Yates has lost her son only a few weeks
after losing a daughter and a granddaughter
in another tragic and cruel accident.
The hearts of all of us go out to her
and her family at this time of their anguish.

Ivan was a close friend of mine for 25 years,
ever since we were undergraduates together.
Even so, I am very conscious of the fact
that no one person could hope to express
the rich variety of affectionate recollection
which all his friends and colleagues have of him.

Ivan had many friends, for he had so many interests
and always made friends. It was of course on the *Observer*
for 14 years that he had the happiest
and most satisfying period of his life as a journalist,
and where his talents were increasingly appreciated.

I cannot speak from inside knowledge of his contribution
to the editorial operations of the *Observer*
but I know how much he loved his work;
I know that David Astor and his colleagues
held him in the warmest esteem and affection.
If I may quote from the tribute in the *Observer*,
so movingly written by Michael Davie:

> Ivan was one of those men whom no newspaper
> should be without – with an astonishing range of
> knowledge and understanding. He had complete
> integrity in his concern for the truth … Almost
> every part of the paper from the Editor
> downwards came to depend on the knowledge
> and judgement of Ivan Yates. He was irreplaceable.

It would be a presumption for me to add anything
to that professional tribute from his fellow journalists.
But Ivan won great *personal* affection,
as well as professional respect.
And it is our memory of him as a *personality*

which we will particularly cherish.
I use the word personality in the true sense of that debased word.

For Ivan conformed to no known social or professional type.
He was always himself, in his own style,
in innumerable distinctive ways: his dress,
his way of speaking, his humour, his courtesy
and his multiplicity of interests
which made him a walking almanac
of esoteric knowledge over an amazing variety of subjects –
from political history and biography
to English country houses and the bench of bishops.

My first enjoyment of Ivan's humour was at Oxford
where he made a hilariously funny speech in the Union,
delivered with immense solemnity, on the motion –
which was perhaps slightly premature in 1951 –
"that this House regrets the decline of the middle classes".

That speech made his name as an undergraduate
and he was elected President of the Union
in what he liked to describe as a vintage year –
his two predecessors in 1951 being Jeremy Thorpe
and William Rees-Mogg.
As Ivan remarked, that trio in one year
suggested a certain catholicity of taste among the voters.

Ivan had a great love of words and of the music
of the English language, both in print and in speech.
He would have loved the beautiful way in which
David Dunhill read the Lesson here today.

Perhaps his first venture into print as a journalist
arose out of an ill-fated try at being a schoolboy actor
in a Christ's Hospital School play,
which for some reason was *Arsenic and Old Lace*.
Ivan played the part of one of the two mad ladies.
The other, as he would recall
with considerable relish, was Bernard Levin.
This remarkable production was only marred
by the unfortunate fact that Ivan,

who was never really at his best
with his hands, was unable at the crucial moment
to get the cork out of the bottle of poison.
The result was that in the next term's play,
which was *Ladies in Retirement*,
Bernard Levin was again in a starring role
but Ivan was asked to write the review
for the school magazine – his first step
towards the journalistic career which
he was to begin ten years later.

At Oxford, Ivan indulged his deep interest in politics
and the Labour Party. His numerous activities,
including those in his college, Pembroke,
left him with practically no leisure time
in which to work for a degree.
As he used to say, the serious illness
which prevented him from taking his final examinations,
came at an extremely opportune moment.

Though he read law and stood once for Parliament,
Ivan gradually abandoned the idea
of a career at the Bar or in politics –
partly perhaps because he was hard up,
partly because journalism offered another way
of involving him with political life,
but perhaps also because Ivan was a gentle man
and did not push his way aggressively in life,
though he had deep principles and deep feelings.
He wrote a long biographical profile (in the *Observer*)
of Hugh Gaitskell, to whose character and cause
he was so strongly drawn.
It was a work of great sensitivity and understanding
which has rarely, if ever, been bettered.

Unlike many people for whom memorial services
are held in church, Ivan was a Christian
both in belief and conduct.
As Jeremy Thorpe said to me the other day,
Ivan Yates never showed or felt any malice.
Though he was a man of deep feeling,

Ivan did not parade the fact.
In that (as in so many other ways)
he was very much an Englishman.
I have in my hand a letter he wrote to me
more than 20 years ago.
It was at a critical moment in my life
and he wanted to say something to raise my spirits:

> As you well know, I've grown up with a peculiarly
> English and wholly wrong-headed habit of not
> expressing anything I feel deeply – but hide it,
> pretend it isn't there. It must be a very tiresome
> habit for my friends – but it has one advantage, that
> when one does say what one feels it means something.

None of us will ever think of him as tiresome.
He had a great gift for making and keeping friends
and for quietly winning the confidence
of those with whom he worked.
It is some tribute perhaps to his remarkable personality
and sense of humour that he got on so well personally
with three somewhat different gentlemen
who were his employers at one time or another,
Randolph Churchill, Lord Beaverbrook and David Astor.

As a journalist his enthusiasm was
in the realm of ideas and opinion.
He did not set himself out to be
the intrepid, swashbuckling front-line reporter.
But he had his moments. From time to time
he went into the field,
without allowing it to change his lifestyle.
Somewhere in Cyprus during an earlier round
of troubles, a convoy of vehicles had been blown up.
In some deserted village in the Troodos mountains
a tall, thin, untidy Englishman
with his spectacles halfway down his nose
came up to a policeman out of the smoke
and said, "Could you possibly direct me
to the best restaurant hereabouts?"

Like all of Ivan's personal friends,
I will always recall his idiosyncrasies with affection.
We shared a flat, went on holidays together.
His own accommodation arrangements tended
to be somewhat sporadic at times,
and he would borrow my house
when my wife and I were abroad.

He was a great man for *outings*.
At any weekend there would come
to any of his friends a cheerful phone call from Ivan
to suggest a drive into the country for lunch.

On one particular occasion, he inveigled my wife and myself
into what may be described as a typical Ivan outing.
There was an excellent lunch at a place
which he had carefully researched,
with a discriminating check on the initials
of those who had made
recommendations in the *Good Food Guide*.
Then to a detailed tour of a stately home
which, of course, happened to be nearby – in this case Cliveden.
"And on our way home," said Ivan, "would you mind
if we took a slight detour?
There's a very interesting monastery
which you might like to look over."

Needless to say, nothing was further from my inclinations
but we went, making a very long detour.
And at the monastery, the conducting monk was somewhat surprised
at the depth of Ivan's informed interest
in his relatively obscure Order.

Ivan was a delightful companion, a fine journalist,
a wise counsellor, a staunch friend.
We shall all miss him very dearly.
Perhaps we shall miss him
for his humour most of all.

7 HEATH TEN, DAY ONE

November 26th, 1975, the Painters' Hall. This was an *Evening Standard* Literary Lunch, the first such occasion I had ever experienced. Literary Lunches are to publicise the sponsoring newspaper and to promote sales of a book. The author makes a speech. He then signs copies of his book which, he hopes, the luncheon guests will queue up to buy.

This Literary Lunch was for two books. One was *Sailing, a Course of My Life* by Mr Edward Heath, MP. The other was by me, *Day by Day – a Dose of My Own Hemlock.* This was a reprint of previous writings, plus a newly written introduction in which I interviewed myself without mercy. (My memoirs, *Grand Inquisitor*, came later in 1989.)

It was only two and a half years since Mr Heath had been Prime Minister. He had lost the Tory leadership to Margaret Thatcher earlier that year, in February 1975, but he had a phenomenal success with his book on sailing. My little book was a much more modest publication. To be coupled at a literary lunch with a famous best-selling author was, of course, a handy boost for me. But when it came to the book-signing after lunch, there was an embarrassingly small queue of purchasers wanting my book. The queue for an autographed copy of the ex-Prime Minister's book was huge.

So that my queue would not dwindle away too quickly, I cleverly prolonged each signing by asking purchasers how they spelt their full names, or by writing in some lengthy expression of greeting and good wishes. I signed one copy for every ten signed by Ted.

The Chairman of the lunch was Sir Max Aitken, son of Lord Beaverbrook who acquired control of the *Evening Standard* in 1923. Like the more famous of the two authors, Sir Max was a well-known yachtsman.

Sir Max, Ladies and Gentlemen:

When I first heard about the arrangements for this luncheon,
I was clearly under the impression that the *Evening Standard*
considered my book to be so remarkable
that a distinguished world statesman
would be speaking in my honour.
But it has slowly dawned upon me
that this lunch is really in honour
of the distinguished world statesman –
because he also happens to have written a book,
not about the great issues of our time,
not disclosing a single Cabinet secret,
not reporting a single slanderous conversation with Cecil King,
but on messing about in boats.
And I would not have dared to use that phrase
had he not used it himself.

In fact, my function here should best be described
as that of a rather superfluous deck-hand.

Sir Max: your father, Lord Beaverbrook,
acquired the *Evening Standard* more than 50 years ago.
We are told by his biographer, Alan Taylor,
that though he wanted political influence
through his mass-circulation papers,
Lord Beaverbrook also wanted *fun*, and the *Evening Standard*
"provided an outlet for his eccentric radicalism".

It would be impertinent of me to suggest,
in Mr Heath's presence, that the combination of authors
chosen for today's lunch is eccentric;
but it is certainly *fun*.
And one might even call it *mischievous*,
which would have greatly pleased Lord Beaverbrook.

I congratulate Mr Heath upon his book about sailing,
without which no Christmas stocking
will be complete this year.
And I congratulate his publisher, Lord Longford,
on producing a best-seller which is so eminently suitable

for decent family reading.[1]
The beautiful illustrations are all in irreproachable taste,
including the handsome semi-nude on page 175
which appears to be Tarzan at the helm
but which you, Sir Max, will easily recognise as yourself.

All I will presume to say in praise of Mr Heath's book
is that it gives as fascinating a picture
of his character and personality
as it does of the sport on which he writes
with such intense enthusiasm.

Some of you may have a technical knowledge of sailing
which is as limited as mine.
It is possible there are those among you
who do not know the difference
between a spinnaker and a spanker.
But even if you do not share
Mr Heath's passion for sailing,
you will feel it on every page of his book;
you will feel the danger, the exhilaration,
the excitement of "the wheel's kick,
and the wind's song and the white sail's shaking".

Students of Mr Heath's political temperament
will be intrigued by the passage where he explains
that, as a yachtsman, he has always concentrated on *racing*.
He has never been inclined to indulge in the less challenging
and less competitive pleasures of *cruising*.
Mr Heath writes (not very convincingly),
"Perhaps, one day, I will take up cruising."
But whatever some people may hope,
there is no sign yet of him cruising in politics.

My sense of inadequacy on this occasion
is increased by the knowledge
that, while I am no expert
on the subject of Mr Heath's book,

[1] Lord Longford was then much in the news as an anti-pornography campaigner.

he is an undoubted expert on the subject of mine,
which is television.

Each of us has his own impressions
of those whom we see on the box.
Whether that impression is due to our own prejudices
or to some mysterious chemistry in the person appearing,
or to some sinister power of the camera,
I do not know, and have given up trying to understand.

Now take Ted Heath. Some people say,
"The trouble with Ted on the telly is he can never be himself."
Others say, with equal conviction, "The trouble with Ted on the telly
is that he cannot be anything *but* himself."

Perhaps it is the softening of my brain
(caused by 20 years in television)
which makes me somewhat slow to understand
how those two theories can be reconciled.

In an interview the other day,
Mr Heath proudly claimed (and I quote),
"No one has ever accused me of being successful on television."
Well, I have a shock for him.
That is precisely the accusation I make today.
The evidence is overwhelming.

The inescapable fact is, that there is now
a constant and insatiable demand for Mr Heath
in every conceivable kind of television programme:
political programmes, music programmes,
sports programmes, book programmes.
Why, the cameras have even pursued him here
to this quiet lunch which he is having
with me and a few friends.

And, mark my words, you'll see him
on all those dreadf... delightful chat shows
which achieve such a high level of conversation.
Already you may have seen Mr Heath
almost dancing down those studio stairs

for an audience with Michael Parkinson,
and doing a sensational double act with Dame Edith Evans.
Before he's finished, he'll be getting
the *Evening Standard* Drama Award.

Next, no doubt, he will be on screen with Russell Harty,
or even David Frost. Indeed, there are no depths
… no heights which Mr Heath may not reach
in his new role as TV star and celebrity author.

I will not abuse your hospitality, Sir Max,
nor the patience of your guests
by referring at length to my book.
May I simply say that it is written in the belief
that someone who works in television
has a duty to ask himself not merely
what that medium *can* do
but what it *ought* to do.
Otherwise one's professional thought and action
will be increasingly governed not by principle or purpose,
but by the mindless mechanics of the medium.

We must restrain and counterbalance the tendencies
inherent in television's coverage of events and issues,
the tendency to distort, to inflame and to trivialise.

There have been great advances,
great achievements in television journalism
over the last 20 years. But it has developed
an increasingly dangerous emphasis on action
(usually violent and bloody action),
on action rather than thought,
on happenings rather than issues,
on shock rather than explanation,
on personalities rather than ideas,
on exposure rather than exposition.
TV is a crude medium, which strikes
at the emotions rather than the intellect.

If our democratic society is to retain

its tradition of reasonableness,
the electronic journalism (which is now
the main mass medium of information)
must do much more than transmit what are known
in the business as "bloody good pictures".

Talking of my book, I think I'm the only person
who has been mugged *twice* this year.
Once by unknown assailants in a street near my home.
And once by Milton Shulman
in the columns of the *Evening Standard.*
That was when he reviewed my book with the savagery
I have always enjoyed so much
when he has directed it at other people.

When apprehended on a charge of reviewing
with intent to inflict his own opinions on the reader,
Mr Shulman asked for numerous other cases
to be taken into consideration.

But today, after this *Evening Standard* lunch,
my heart is full of forgiveness.
I am particularly delighted that Mr Charles Wintour,
the Editor of the *Evening Standard,*
is here, following his recent holiday in China.
We all enjoyed those brilliant articles of his which
he managed to persuade his Features Editor to publish.

Mr Wintour's visit was regarded as highly significant
in the People's Republic of China.
On many a lip in Peking is heard the old Chinese proverb
which freely translated says, "If Wintour comes,
can Shulman be far behind?"

Sir Max, thank you for presiding. Ladies and Gentlemen, thank you.

8   A TWO-SENTENCE TOAST

February 11th, 1976 at the home of the Rt Hon Christopher Chataway. I was speaking as the Best Man at his wedding to Carola Walker which had taken place that morning. I was given this honour partly because of my long friendship with Chris, which dated back to our days together at ITN in the mid-'50s, and partly because I had something to do with his having met Carola in the first place.

After the simple ceremony in Kensington Town Hall there was a small, quiet lunch with family and friends at which I was asked to speak – on condition that I said only a few – a very few – words.

With characteristic self-discipline, I obeyed, albeit reluctantly, their strict injunction not to speak at length. Their reasonable assumption was that the less time I had, the less indiscreet I could become. This stratagem did not entirely defeat me.

For both bride and groom it was their second marriage. I am glad to say that they are, in 1999, still happily married with two fine sons, Adam and Matthew Chataway.

Ladies and Gentlemen:

I have been asked to speak on this happy occasion.
To be accurate, I have been asked to utter
not more than two sentences.
Eventually I accepted,
after the traditional show of reluctance,
only when it was explained
that I was being relied upon because
of the good taste for which I am renowned.

My first duty, for the benefit of those who were not present,
is to report to you that Carola and Christopher
were lawfully wedded in Kensington Town Hall
at dawn this morning.

The condemned m... the bridegroom was calm
throughout the proceedings, which went without a hitch.
It was a short and simple ceremony,
with its own unpretentious dignity.
I can only describe it as
rather like getting a new parking permit.

But it was a deeply moving, and very human moment –
the middle-aged banker with his beautiful child bride.
It was especially moving for me,
for it was I who first introduced them
one fateful morning high in the Swiss Alps.
In the words of a romantic song,
popular when Chris's mother and I were in our teens:

What e'er befall I still recall
That sunlit mountain scene.

The introduction, of course, came about when I,
with characteristic generosity, was giving them the benefit
of my skill and experience as a skier.
One always likes to help beginners on the slopes.
But little did I realise what they were beginning
and on what slippery slope they were beginning to slide.

In the mountain resort of Verbier,
there is now a new ski run –
of a most precipitous and exciting kind –
which is marked, "This way to Kensington Register Office".

That ends the second of my two sentences,
and I offer to Chris and Carola
my love and congratulations.

I would only venture to express the hope,
with all the good taste at my command,
that I will not be called upon to perform
this function for either of them again.

To the health and happiness of Carola and Chris.

9   THE OYSTER FEAST

October 29th, 1976, the Colchester Oyster Feast in the Town Hall. This was an invitation which I accepted for personal nostalgia. When I was a teenager and a young man, Colchester was the town nearest my home. I had heard of the famous annual Oyster Feast when I was a boy, but had never thought I would one day be invited.

The ritual includes a special train for the hour's journey to Colchester. Among the guests are leading parliamentarians and public figures, actors and actresses and the inevitable television personalities. The host or hostess is the Mayor.

The lunch is well named a Feast. There were unlimited oysters. I had, if my recollection is correct, four dozen. This was only because other guests, I am glad to say, were allergic to oysters.

By happy chance I was able to quote in this speech a personal telegram to me from the former Prime Minister Harold Macmillan. Only a few days before this Oyster Feast a TV interview by me with Mr Macmillan made big front-page headlines. Mr Macmillan was making his first entry into current politics since his resignation in 1963. Supermac's comeback had come after 13 years. Hence the witty telegram about Rip Van Winkle in this Oyster Feast speech. Rip Van Winkle, whose fabled adventures were published by the house of Macmillan, came back after 20 years' sleep.

The one drawback was the number of guest speakers. There were seven. I was the seventh, called on at nearly 4pm. The first speaker had been the Duke of Kent, who did not exactly bring the house down. By the time I rose to speak, the audience, stuffed full of delicious oysters and copiously supplied with excellent wine, was past wanting to hear anything, let alone anything too heavy.

Madam Mayor, My Lords, Ladies and Gentlemen:

There must be some mistake.
My name is Yarwood. I have been asked
to conclude the cabaret on this occasion.

Of course, if there is an overwhelming demand
to do a boring impersonation of Robin Day
(and I usually find there is),
I shall respond to the popular will.
Robin Day is about the only one I've got left now.
Harold's gone, Ted's gone, Jeremy's gone.

However, Mr Day is annoyed with me
because I get paid more for impersonating him
than he gets for being himself.
So much for the social contract.

But if it's Mr Day you want, so be it.

I assume that the idea of having me as the seventh speaker
was to end with something light and carefree.
If anyone can think of anything
to be light and carefree about,
I'd be glad to know what it is.

And why ask *me* to be light and carefree?
I'm not one of those broadcasters
who bring laughter into your hearts
or happiness into your homes.

How I would like to be one of those celebrity interviewers,
whose dreadf... delightful late-night chat-shows
make them stars of the entertainment world.

How lovely to have the gift of Michael Parkinson
or Russell Harty to make your studio guests
seem almost as celebrated and beautiful as yourself.

Following the sensational success
of my recent interview with the ex-Prime Minister,

I have decided not to interview
any politician under 82 years old.

Incidentally, that interview with Mr Macmillan[1]
made such big headlines the other day
because it was his return to politics after 13 years.
Immediately he saw the headline Mr Macmillan
promptly sent me this charming telegram:

> Rip Van Winkle never had it
> so good on the front pages.

It is a great pleasure to be responding for the guests.
My special pleasure in so doing,
of which you may be unaware,
is that I am almost a native of Colchester.

Colchester is the town I knew best in my boyhood.
Because my home was for many years at West Mersea –
where, of course, the *best* oysters come from.

Colchester was the town where I enlisted in the army.
And I am proud to tell you that in the dark days of the war
I served with a devotion to duty,
which modesty prevents me from describing in detail,
in the West Mersea Home Guard.

I have never been able to convince my wife
(she was born in the summer of 1940)
that *Dad's Army*, far from being a comedy,
is a documentary of great historical authenticity.

Thank you, Madam Mayor, for your splendid hospitality,
for your patriotic decision at this time
of crisis and retrenchment
to raise the number of speeches to seven ...
and to reduce the number of courses to four.
For, as we have been authoritatively told,[2]

[1] Interview transmitted October 20th, 1976.

[2] By Labour Cabinet Minister Tony Crosland.

"the party is over".
We are at the end of the road.
We cannot go on like this.

And as the seventh speaker at this Feast, I will not go on either.

In my profession I have learned to obey
the 11th commandment, which the Almighty made
when he invented television:
Thou shalt not overrun thy three minutes.

So on behalf of the guests, may I respond
with warmest appreciation of the toast and your hospitality.

10 SHUT UP AND LISTEN

November 30th, 1976, Grosvenor House Hotel. This was the annual banquet, ball and fund-raising jamboree – complete with bingo – of the Grand Order of Water Rats. This curiously named organisation includes among its members stars of the entertainment world, variety artists, comedians, singers, performers of many kinds. Royalty and other public figures accept honorific appointment in the Order. Prince Philip and Prince Charles are Companion Rats. The Water Rats, founded over 100 years ago, raise money for charity and do much good work.

I had been asked to "reply for the guests after dinner". Another speaker was Lord Shinwell, then aged 92.

No one had bothered to inform me that the proceedings, which began at 7.30pm, consisted of much more than drinks, dinner and speeches. My speech was indeed to be "after dinner" – more than two *hours* after dinner. Between dinner and me there was fund-raising bingo, a ceremonial procession and numerous other goings-on peculiar to the Grand Order of Water Rats.

The audience of over 1,500 in the great ballroom of Grosvenor House had become more rowdy as the evening wore on. I did not rise until after 11pm. By then, the time had passed for my "after-dinner" speech. But I had no option but to press on, and to disregard the noise and chatter of the audience. This got worse. It was an uphill fight. After a time I shouted back at them to shut up and listen.

At this I was loudly cheered. This meant the rowdiness was from a minority, although it had seemed widespread. Anyway, eventually there was reasonable quiet. They were listening, and laughing.

Some of the well-known entertainers were clearly embarrassed that I had initially been received with less than customary courtesy to a guest. The head Water Rat (or King Rat as he is called) thanked me effusively and apologetically. He added that I would be invited the following year simply to enjoy myself, without having, he said, to sing for my supper. No such invitation came.

At the end I got a standing ovation. Whether from sympathy or from admiration, I could only guess.

Your Majesty King Rat, Prince Rat, Companion Rats,
Ratlings and any other vermin which may have got in:

I want to thank Mr Tommy Trinder,
now that the speeches are over,
for calling on me to open the cabaret.

I know how good my impersonations are,
but I never thought I would reach such perfection
as actually to be introduced as Robin Day
on such an occasion as this.

Mr Day will not be pleased. He has already written to the BBC,
complaining bitterly about me:
"How do you justify paying Mike Yarwood more
for impersonating me than I get for being myself?
What sort of incomes policy is that?"

But, of course, if there is an overwhelming demand
for me to give you one of my boring impersonations of Mr Day
(and I usually find that there is) then I will.
As long as no one wants me to do Margaret Thatcher.
I'm having rather a struggle with her and I'm losing.
So now it's your favourite and my favourite – Robin Day.

Let me assure you, *money* is not my object.
The BBC is a non-profit-making public service
and assumes that most of its contributors
work on the same principle.
You will all be familiar with that memorable message
to the BBC's Artistes' Contracts Department
from Mr Bill Cotton:

   Small is beautiful.

No – what *I* am after is not money,
but a new dimension to my image.
Ladies and gentlemen, I want to be loved.
If Kojak can be loved, why can't I?
I've even thought of shaving off my hair.
Or of offering the Prime Minister a lollipop.

I am afraid that by inviting me tonight,
the Grand Order of Water Rats has invited the wrong kind of man.
I am, alas, not one of those celebrity interviewers
whose dreadf… delightful late-night chat-shows
make them glamorous stars of the entertainment world.

What a gift it must be to make your studio guests
seem almost as celebrated and beautiful as yourself.
How lucky the chat-show merchants are!
By talking to such beautiful and charming people,
they begin to look beautiful and charming themselves.

If only I could be like Russell Harty,
who can make himself look young
simply by talking to Lana Turner or Margaret Duchess of Argyll.

If only I could be like Michael Parkinson,
glowing with the reflected charisma
of a sex symbol from the world of sport,
such as George Best or Ted Heath.

If only I could be like David Frost.
What must it be like to have the sort of personality
that can make Clive Jenkins walk out of a television studio?

Not that I have anything against these TV chat-shows.
I just think they are the least satisfying form
of oral intercourse yet practised by civilised man.

Your Majesty King Rat:
I can only interpret your invitation to me
as one more sign of the nation's grim mood[1]
in these desperate times. Last year it was different.
Your guest of honour was the then Prime Minister.[2]
But now you have obviously decided
that the time for frivolity is past.

[1] The topical background was the Labour Government's battle against soaring inflation, which had risen the previous year to 27 per cent.
[2] Harold Wilson, but he had resigned earlier that year and was succeeded by Jim Callaghan.

Even to be a guest of the Water Rats makes me feel full of sadness.
Standing here amid the glittering stars
of humour and entertainment,
I am conscious of my life's biggest regret:
that I never became a music-hall entertainer.
For that was always my secret dream.
Not that I dreamt of being anything spectacular or brilliant.
Just a simple, straightforward combination
of Eric Morecambe and Des O'Connor,
and, to give me some class, a touch of Schnozzle Durante.

Alas, it was not to be. Perhaps I should be thankful.
Take the great comedians,
the comic geniuses of stage and screen.
Behind their professional facade of fun,
they are wretched, miserable, anxiety-ridden creatures.
Where is their next joke to come from?
Even worse, where is their next *new* joke to come from?
Where are their new scripts, their new gag-writers,
their new songs? How long can they count
on the public's fickle affection?

With me, it is precisely the reverse.
Whatever may be my professional exterior,
you will find that underneath, inside, deep down,
I am happy and joyful, light-hearted and carefree.
I do not have the worries of the comedian or entertainer.
I never make jokes, so I don't have to worry
where my new ones are coming from.

My business is crisis, so I don't have to worry
about running short of material.
I am blissfully happy in the certain knowledge
that an unending flow of disaster and conflict
can be relied upon to keep me busy indefinitely.

So to the Water Rats and the stars who are their guests,
I say this: your scriptwriters will fail you,
your hairlines will recede, your chins will sag,
your jokes will lose their antique charm.
But events will never let *me* down.

I can always rely on human nature to be appalling.

History is my scriptwriter. Politics is my choreographer.
Disaster is my accompanist. Inflation is my inspiration.
So, Ladies and Gentlemen, rest assured that many a year from now
I will still be at it.

Which brings me back to
the speech I am supposed to be making
on behalf of your celebrated guests.
Let me take back every word
I said about entertainers fading away.
Because, of course, they are, all of them,
stars who will glitter indefinitely.
One of them[1] is truly ageless and immortal.
She is

    yours till the stars lose their glory
    yours till the birds fail to sing.
    They'll be happy to know
    that as I saw you go,
    you were singing this song.

Let me end – on a note of gravity –
with some words which enshrine my philosophy of life,
words which are as unforgettable
as they are incomprehensible:

    Inka–dinka dee kadinkadoo kadinkadee …[2]

---

[1] Dame Vera Lynn, created DBE (belatedly) the previous year.

[2] With arms outstretched, Schnozzle Durante-style.

April 9th, 1978, St Catherine's College, Oxford. The annual Anglo-German "Königswinter" conferences are held in alternate years at Königswinter on the Rhine near Bonn, or in either Oxford or Cambridge. In 1978 Königswinter was in St Catherine's College, Oxford, whose starkly modern architecture was not to everyone's taste.

My function was to be the *rapporteur* of one of the four discussion groups into which the delegates were divided. One of my fellow *rapporteurs* was Douglas Hurd, MP, then Tory back-bencher in opposition, who later became Foreign Secretary.

It is a Königswinter tradition that the *rapporteur*'s summing-up should be not only fair, but entertaining. Wit is not discouraged. The British, on the whole, tend to be wittier than the Germans.

My audience were the Königswinter delegates, consisting, as usual, of over 100 parliamentarians, Cabinet Ministers, editors, officials, academics, broadcasters, economists and industrialists from both countries.

My group had discussed for a total of several hours over two days. But the *rapporteur* had to do his duty. I was up wrestling with mine for most of the previous night, and I missed two of the evening receptions which are such an enjoyable feature of Königswinter conferences.

I was lucky. Though the group's discussions had not been very exciting, there had been one or two happenings. Of these I made the most when, as *rapporteur*, I summed up the discussions of Group III to the final session of the full conference.

Mr Chairman:

It all began quite peacefully —
a typical Friday afternoon at a Königswinter conference.

The distinguished members of Group III
had abandoned their constituents, their ministries, their students,

their businesses, their readers, to sit around a table discussing
the far-reaching question, "How well is democracy working?"
It was a question to which they all knew the short answer.

Nonetheless, it was a question which raised great themes,
high principles and fundamental issues.
Not for Group III the grey technicalities
of European monetary union, or the neutron bomb, or mass
unemployment.
Group III were dealing with grander, broader themes:
freedom, order, humanity, youth, women.
And at one point (thanks to Sir Robert Birley) the divine right of kings.

For some time the discussion meandered along
as calmly and as sluggishly as the River Cherwell.
The exchanges were quiet and courteous.
Attention occasionally wandered.
The skill of the two interpreters was much admired,
although sometimes I thought there was clearly a case
for *three* interpreters – one for German, one for English
and one for Sociology.

Heads, I regret to say, momentarily nodded at the beginning.
One member dreamt that he was in Group II
arguing that the neutron bomb was an inconvenient weapon
to drop on St Catherine's College,
because it would destroy the people and not the buildings.

Then suddenly, with an almighty splash,
a hand-grenade was tossed in by a young activist
disguised as the Editor of a respected British weekly.
His explosive intervention not only shook up,
but lit up, the discussion.
It was a ferocious onslaught on the British Parliament
and its members, several of whom were present.
They did not recover until the following morning.

As the dust settled, the members of Group III
were able to study the Englishman[1]

---

[1] Mr Andrew Knight, then Editor of *The Economist*.

who had resorted to such indiscriminate,
but clearly well-planned, brutality.
He was obviously an intellectual, though he looked extremely civilised.
He had short hair and was neatly dressed and well-spoken.
His English was almost as good as that of Professor Dahrendorf.

So far as one could tell, he came
from a prosperous and privileged middle-class background.
There was speculation, from social psychologists present,
that he suffered from a guilt complex
about his sumptuous way of life in a penthouse in St James's, W1.

Be that as it may, it was what he said that shocked.
"No one," he declared (and I quote), "gives a fig for Parliament.
Parliament does not really exist.
Parliament does not really matter.
The two-party system has frozen Parliament
in aspic by the lack of proportional representation."
Then with a breathtaking but bewildering change of metaphor
he said, "The mother of Parliaments has become a spinster."

One of his most wounding remarks, delivered with a cold unconcern
for the feelings of those present,
was that there is "no sight so demeaning
as that of a British back-bench MP
hanging about for years,
waiting for promotion to ministerial office
and being whipped through the voting lobbies".

Several Honourable gentlemen around the Group III table
fitted that description quite closely.
You would have been proud of them.
Their bearing under fire
would have done credit to the Brigade of Guards.
No rhinoceroses, Mr Chairman, have thicker hides.
They did not wince as the lash was falling.
Their upper lips were uniformly stiff.

Not until next morning was there retaliation from the British side.
The young editor's onslaught on Parliament
was condemned by another British journalist

as "wild and irresponsible" and as "the kind of talk
which could lead to young people turning to terrorism".

One well-known Conservative MP[1] gave evidence
of his own excellent record as a Member of Parliament.
He appeared to be reading out extracts
from the draft of his election address
at the forthcoming general election.
He pointed out that in championing
his constituency's interests he had once made
the longest speech in Parliament for 140 years.
His audience in Group III were grateful
for his relative self-restraint on this occasion.

As the argument swung to and fro,
the interesting fact became clear
that there was much more concern among the British
about the working of ancient democratic institutions here,
than there was among the Germans about
the new democratic institutions in Germany.

The argument about Parliamentary government
was brought to a more lucid conclusion
by Professor Ralf Dahrendorf, who said,
"The dangerous immobility of both our democracies
lies in the prevailing political orthodoxy
of the *centre* which permeates our institutions."
Inevitably that brought talk of reconstruction
and even of destruction.
One could begin to see the link with terrorism.

At that point Group III
turned to that very subject as its second theme –
the use of criminal violence in appalling and atrocious ways
to achieve political and social ends.

The discussion on terrorism began with an analysis
of the German experience by a British expert,

---

[1] Sir Bernard Braine, MP.

General Clutterbuck.[1] He traced the escalation
of the German terrorism, graduating (as he put it)
from student demonstrations originally,
then to attacks on capitalist property,
then to bombing of an indiscriminate nature against people,
then to assassination and then kidnapping.
Each stage more brutal, more ruthless,
more sophisticated than the last.

Why had there been no similar escalation in Britain?
Why had the Angry Brigade not developed
a second generation to become
something like Baader-Meinhof?
General Clutterbuck's opinion was that the British political system
gave scope for extremist groups
to work within, or at least to influence,
the main political parties and trade unions.

But he went further than that.
He expressed an opinion which was the second bombshell
of our group's deliberations.
Having praised the stability and continuity
provided by the German constitution and electoral system,
he went on, "If we in Britain want to enjoy
the same stability and continuity,
we must be prepared to pay the price,
24 lives perhaps, of having
Baader-Meinhof-type terrorism to go with it."
I cannot report to you the reactions
of various captains of industry and other public figures
sitting round the table
whose lives might be part of the price thus to be paid.

It's incredible to report
that there was no comment
on General Clutterbuck's interesting argument.
Perhaps everyone was simply struck dumb with amazement.
Perhaps nobody took his arguments seriously.

---

[1] Major-General Richard Clutterbuck, CB, OBE, Colonel-Commandant Royal Engineers, lecturer at Exeter University.

Several speakers, both German and British,
emphasised how bafflingly complex
were the causes and motivations of terrorism.
There was the motivation of the young black student in South Africa,
denied not only the basic civil rights
but any hope of obtaining them peacefully.
A German speaker referred to the quite different motivation
expressed by a young girl terrorist in Germany.
She said she had turned to terrorism
because she had been bored
by eating so much caviare at her father's table.
Perhaps the most disturbing disclosure
was that at a recent conference on terrorism in Hamburg,
a Bavarian government official expressed the opinion
that one cause of German terrorism
was a book on social conflict written 20 years ago
by a German sociologist called Ralf Dahrendorf!

Finally, the discussion on terrorism raised one of the questions
on which most of us in the group
felt totally unqualified to pronounce.
There were not many such questions.
Why was there a much higher proportion of women
in terrorist gangs than in other activities in society?
The British expert in terrorism (General Clutterbuck)
was ready with an explanation.
He drew a parallel with women's love of riding
and explained (I think I quote him correctly),
"Women like to have a grip
on something powerful, like a horse, or a gun."
At this (unknown to us in Group III)
there was a loud burst of laughter in Group I
from the Editor of the London *Daily Telegraph*.[1]
He had accidentally tuned in to our Group III on his headphones.
I am glad to say that he was immediately rebuked
by the puzzled chairman of Group I for his inexplicable behaviour.

The chairman of Group III immediately proposed

---

[1] Then the Rt Hon William Deedes, MC, former Conservative Cabinet Minister, now Lord Deedes.

that "women in society" should be a major theme
at next year's Königswinter,
and that this would require more women at Königswinter.
As the applause for this suggestion died away,
the only lady member of Group III reminded us
that in her home country of Northern Ireland
the only helpful and exciting development of recent years
had been the peace movement launched by two courageous women.
Group III then disbanded with their male chauvinist tails between
    their legs.

12 MY FIRST 25 YEARS ON TV

O ctober 15th, 1980, BBC Television Centre. This was a dinner kindly given by my old friend and colleague Sir Ian Trethowan, then Director-General of the BBC, to mark my 25 years in television. *The Times* informed its readers that morning as follows:

> Tonight Robin Day will receive the BBC's supreme
> accolade of a private dinner party with Sir Ian Trethowan,
> the D-G, even though it was the rival Independent
> Television News that gave Day his big break.

My television career had begun when ITN started in 1955. The 40 dinner guests included some from that period of my life.

The dinner took place on a night of intense political excitement. Earlier that very evening, Jim Callaghan had resigned as Labour Party leader.[1] And one of the guests at the dinner was Denis Healey, a leading contender for the succession to Mr Callaghan. Among the other parliamentarians were Edward Heath, Shirley Williams, Enoch Powell and Jo Grimond. Also present, in addition to senior BBC figures, were my old friends Bernard Levin, Bob McKenzie, Christopher Chataway, Ludovic Kennedy, Michael Charlton, Sir Geoffrey Cox, George Ffitch, Keith Kyle, Bob Carvel and Mr Justice Waterhouse, whose memorable contribution to my career is mentioned in this speech.

Chairman, Director-General, Ladies and Gentlemen:

It is a very great honour to be present
at this memorial serv... celebration dinner.

I am naturally unnerved to be addressing
this glittering company of parliamentarians,

---

[1] Having been Prime Minister, 1976–79.

opinion-formers, pontificators, senior BBC executives
(several of whom I can recognise),
not to mention long-suffering colleagues
and friends who know far too much about me.

I am deeply grateful to Mr Heath –
I thank him warmly for his generous remarks tonight,
especially because I well remember
what he has said about me in the past.

To Mr Healey I am also grateful, not only for speaking so kindly,
but for coming here on this particular night
when he would surely much prefer
to be enjoying the camaraderie of his Party colleagues.
I have affectionate memories of many interviews with him.
He has always seemed to like them
and has never insulted me more than once
in any single interview.

Which brings me to the real purpose of tonight's gathering.
Ostensibly it is a flattering tribute.
In reality it is a subtle hint that "enough is enough".
You are all here tonight
so that I may announce my long-awaited decision.

The time has now come to end the weeks
of malicious speculation and rumour,
largely engineered by Professor Robert McKenzie
(who has been urging me to make way for an older man),
and by David Dimbleby, who regards me
(if I may use the phrase in his presence)
as one of Yesterday's Men.[1]

At this point, may I tell Miss Joan Marsden[2]
it's no good her giving me time-signals.
I'm certainly not ignoring them. That has never happened.

[1] Yesterday's Men was the title of David Dimbleby's TV film (June 1971) about Labour leaders in opposition which enfuriated Harold Wilson.

[2] Doyenne of floor-managers in the BBC TV studios, known to all as "Mother".

It's just that my eyes are misted over with emotion.
Joan is only one of several ladies here
under whose lash I have slaved
for much of my television life.
I pay grateful tribute to those gifted producers,
Margaret Douglas and Barbara Maxwell.
Beneath their feminine charm
they conceal a ruthless capacity
for manipulating men like me, who have been their puppets.

And Diana Edwards-Jones.
She is the award-winning ITN director now devoting
all her talents to making Alastair Burnet
a worthy successor to Reginald Bosanquet.
But in 1955 Diana had an even more difficult task:
working with me on those very early ITN bulletins
which were a constant reproach to those
who did not believe in miracles.

Then there is that great lady, Grace Wyndham Goldie.
I salute her as a brilliant and creative pioneer,
who foresaw sooner and more clearly than anyone
the impact which television would have on our democracy.
I am deeply indebted to her
for all her critical advice and penetrating wisdom.
The best example of her judgment
was when I first applied
for a job on BBC Television in 1954.
She took me at my face value – and sent me to radio.

It was when I was in radio that I got a 'phone call.
The call was from someone at this table.
But for him I would never have got into television.
So he may have a lot on his conscience.
I refer to Sir Ronald Waterhouse,
who is now one of Her Majesty's judges.
We were called to the Bar together
on the same night in the Middle Temple.
He, unlike me, was clearly destined for the glittering prizes.
I was soon to fall by the wayside
and to become a failed barrister.

One summer's afternoon in 1955,
Ronald rang me at Broadcasting House.
I had become a BBC Radio Talks producer –
temporary, acting and virtually unpaid.
He told me of an advertisement by something called
Independent Television News
(of which I had never heard)
on Gray's Inn notice-board.
It invited members of the Bar to apply to be
one of ITN's first "newscasters", whatever that meant.

I did an audition, which was ghastly, but I got the job –
for reasons which have never been clear to me.
I was very lucky. Lucky especially because the other newscaster
was some sort of national celebrity and sex symbol,
though completely unknown to me.
He was a healthy, clean-limbed youth,
who seemed to have a strongbut wholesome appeal
to women viewers in particular.
He got £1,500 per annum. I got £1,000, which he thought fair.
And because of Chris Chataway
nobody paid attention to my start in TV, which was just as well.

As time went on, I moved over to *Panorama* and the BBC
for the next 21 years.
I was often accused, believe it or not, of rudeness to politicians.
But that was before Parliament could be heard on radio.
That made everybody realise how polite and deferential
I had always been to our rulers.

Ian, you have done me great honour.
I particularly appreciate the special courtesy of your invitation to
    my wife,
Katherine, on this otherwise spouseless occasion.

I apologise to all those whom I have not had time to insult.

You, Sir Ian, have given a splendid dinner.
There may be better ways of spending
the licence-holders' money,
but I can't for the moment think of any.

You may rest assured that I will continue
 to be inspired by that simple motto
(which has sometimes led me to the brink of trouble),
the words of Montaigne
(which for greater clarity I shall translate):
"Sit he on never so high a throne,
a man still sits on his own bottom."

Sir Ian, Ladies and Gentlemen, thank you very much.

A HERETIC ON LIBEL

December 5th, 1980, Cumberland Lodge, Windsor Great Park. This was one of the weekend seminars held by the Inner Temple for Bar students and young barristers. Also present were judges and Benchers of the Inn.

The subject of the seminar was "Press Freedom: Libel, Contempt and Confidentiality".

As a broadcaster who was once at the Bar, I was asked to make the keynote address at this weekend seminar. I have reprinted here the main part of my remarks, namely the part concerned with the law of libel, which is the most entertaining of the three topics. I wanted to explain why I did not (and still do not) share the view fashionable in media circles that our libel laws are illiberal and draconian. I rather suspect that the opposite view was expected from me.

My talk on libel concentrated on two central questions: Is press freedom unduly restricted? And should libel juries be abolished? I did not deal with the whole law of libel in this keynote address. It was not "libel law in a nutshell".

Both in case law and by statute, the law of libel has developed considerably since 1980. Even so, I do not now retreat from the main principles I was defending then. I still maintain that our law of libel is, broadly speaking, fair and reasonable, and that the balance between protecting a person's reputation and protecting press freedom is about right.

I am still against any so-called reform in the libel law which could make it easier for the media to defame people with impunity. And I am still strongly in favour of keeping juries in libel cases.

The audience was as learned as it was lively. Among the senior participants were Mr Justice Comyn, Mr Justice Neill, co-author of a famous libel textbook, and Judge Hawser, QC.

Judge Hawser, Ladies and Gentlemen:

I must have accepted this invitation in a moment
when the balance of my mind was disturbed.
Because the nearer tonight came,
the more I realised how unsuitable I was
to talk on three complex legal subjects
to a gathering of judges, and barristers,
and (even more formidable) Bar students,
with their enthusiastic brains sizzling with the learned academic
subtleties of the *Law Quarterly Review*,
or the latest revolutionary utterance by Lord Denning.

For I am merely a failed barrister who has managed to do better
at the much easier occupation into which I drifted –
that of television. I am grateful to Master Roskill
for correcting the error on your agenda
which alleges that I am a member of the Inner Temple.
I am of the Middle.
Naturally I took eminent counsel's opinion
as to whether this was a libel on me or on the Inner Temple.
His answer did not encourage me to issue a writ.

My pupil master in 1952 was Lord Justice Lawton (as he now is).[1]
Whatever my shortcomings as a pupil,
he is nowadays kind enough to see me
retrospectively in a more flattering light,
as he does with another of his pupils
who has done quite well in another field,
Mrs Margaret Thatcher. But Lord Justice Lawton
accepts no responsibility except for the good qualities
of the Prime Minister and of myself,
whatever those qualities may be.

I even made a few promising appearances in the courts.
One of my more notable triumphs
was before that august tribunal, the Carshalton Magistrates Court.
I successfully defended a lorry-driver

[1] The Rt Hon Sir Frederick Lawton, who retired in 1986.

on a charge of indecent exposure.
Considerations of time and good taste
prevent me from giving you the full flavour
of that case in all its detail.
Enough to say I fully expected
to become standing counsel
for the Transport and General Workers' Union.

But now, 27 years later, such knowledge of the law
as I had has been lost in the mists of time.
So in front of this learned and distinguished audience
I speak with even more than my usual humility.

I stand before you as nothing more
than the reasonable media man.

I cannot offer you a profound or scholarly address
on these fascinating areas of the law.
Permit me to present a few thoughts,
with emphasis on topicality,
as a working journalist and broadcaster.

So far as *libel* is concerned, my personal experience
as a broadcasting journalist has been extremely unusual
if not unique.
Unlike any newspaper journalist and unlike broadcasters
whose work is mainly pre-recorded, or scripted,
much of my television and radio work
has been "live", unscripted and off-the-cuff.

Once on the air in those circumstances
I have been totally unprotected
by libel lawyers, editors or sub-editors.
So what is called the "autonomy of the instant voice"
has required a fairly keen and immediate instinct
for what may be libel or contempt.

I am a heretic on libel because most members
of my profession protest about how much our libel law
restricts the freedom of the media to expose –
what we call investigative journalism

but what the Americans call
by the good old English word "muck-raking".
That criticism of the libel law is voiced
not only by most journalists,
but by some distinguished lawyers.

My heretical position is that the law of libel
is, on balance and broadly speaking, fair and reasonable.
The balance between protecting a person's reputation
and protecting press freedom is in my opinion just about right.

I am against any change in the libel law
which could make it easier for the media
to defame people with impunity.
And I am strongly against abolition of juries in libel cases.

Consider one of the main changes which is proposed
to liberate the shackled media;
this was restated the other day by a leading solicitor
who is an expert libel practitioner,
Mr Peter Carter-Ruck.
He advocated a new defence of qualified privilege for the press:
"The extension of qualified privilege
to the publication in good faith
of matters of public interest based on evidence
which might reasonably be believed to be true."

With respect to Mr Carter-Ruck,
I can see no convincing grounds
for introducing such a defence.
If *Private Eye*, or the *Sunday Mirror*, or *The Times*,
or the BBC, publishes about you
a disgraceful falsehood in "good faith",
on evidence which might reasonably have been believed,
why should that destroy your right
to compensation for grave damage to your reputation?

Supposing we did have this defence for newspapers?
Take the recent affair of the *Sunday Mirror* and its allegation
that Prince Charles and Lady Diana Spencer
had met secretly on the Royal Train,

with the obvious implication that this alleged secret meeting
in the middle of the night was for a purpose
other than to discuss the Minimum Lending Rate.
Should we really change the law
so that the Editor of the *Sunday Mirror*
could claim qualified privilege
by showing that he published in good faith
and with reasonable grounds for believing
that his evidence was impeccably reliable?
My simple view is that a newspaper should not be able
to get away with it by proving,
if it can, that they honestly believed
on reasonable grounds that a libel was true.

Let us take a matter in which *The Times*
was involved, much to its discredit.

A few years ago *The Times* published
as a front-page story the suggestion
that a Cambridge don called Mr Donald Beves
had been involved with Burgess, Maclean and Philby.
Mr Beves was dead, so libel did not arise.

But even if Mr Beves had still been alive
The Times might well have published it
if (and this is the point) the law of libel
had been changed to permit the defence
of qualified newspaper privilege, as proposed
by Mr Carter-Ruck and some newspaper editors.

What justice would there have been for Mr Beves
if, having been branded in effect
a Communist homosexual traitor,
he could get no redress
because *The Times* had been able to prove
that their monumental cock-up
had been made honestly and on reasonable grounds?

So I am against that proposed defence.

Now why am I against the abolition of libel juries?

First because the issues which a jury decides
in a libel case are more suited for a jury's decision
than for professional adjudication by a judge,
however expert and experienced he may be
in deciding damages in other kinds of action.

Whether a plaintiff's reputation has been damaged
or his honour impugned, and how seriously,
are questions which may involve all kinds
of political, social, industrial or moral considerations
which are better assessed by a random group of 12 citizens
than by a professional judge, however learned and experienced.

And I suspect that many judges would prefer
that the buck is passed to the jury.

Was not a jury better suited than a judge
to decide whether one political buccaneer had libelled another?
(I'm thinking of RANDOLPH CHURCHILL
and GERALD NABARRO,
or was it the other way round?)
Or whether PROFESSOR HAROLD LASKI
had been libelled by the *Newark Advertiser*?

Or whether LIBERACE had been libelled by CASSANDRA?[1]
The celebrated *Daily Mirror* columnist
described the American entertainer in words
which rank as the most enjoyable libel of all time:

>   this deadly, winking, sniggering,
>   snuggling, chromium-plated,
>   scent-impregnated, luminous, quivering, giggling,
>   fruit-flavoured, mincing, ice-covered
>   heap of mother-love

Mr Justice Salmon left the jury to decide

---

[1] This was in 1956, long before Liberace (who died of Aids) was acknowledged as a homosexual. Cassandra did not attempt to "justify", ie to prove that Liberace was homosexual, so the jury did not have to decide whether he was or not.

whether these words could connote homosexuality,
except for one word which he ruled, curiously enough,
could *not* connote homosexuality: "fruit-flavoured"!

Another reason for keeping juries
is that the essential question in libel
(here may I adopt the words of LORD DEVLIN)
is, "What is the meaning
that the words convey to the ordinary man?"

It seems to me better that this question
should be answered by ordinary lay citizens
rather than lawyers. But in saying that, I do *not* believe,
as many people believe, including even some lawyers,
that judges are somehow withdrawn
and isolated from ordinary life.

The judges whom I happen to know personally
all strike me as ordinary human beings,
some of them rather *too* ordinary.
Some of them are so ordinary
as to be extremely worried about becoming bankrupt
as a result of going on to the bench.

And I have no doubt that most judges
are capable of judging
what the meaning of words is to ordinary men.

So why do I think it is better
for juries to decide than judges?
Simply because in libel cases
justice is more clearly seen to be done
by a jury of 12 ordinary citizens
than by one High Court judge.
This is because the balance
between protecting an individual's reputation
and upholding freedom of speech
is a matter which lies at the heart
of our constitutional rights and liberties
and one in which ordinary lay citizens
should be seen to be involved.

The argument for abolishing juries is often based
on the allegedly excessive damages
which juries are apt to award.
This myth seems to be widely accepted as true.
I look forward to hearing in later discussion
which awards by juries can really be said
to have been outrageously high.
I can hear (or I ought to be able to hear)
someone murmuring,
"What about LEWIS and the *Daily Telegraph*?"
"What about the PQ 17 case?[1] What about KOJAK?"

Well, in the Lewis case, huge damages of £217,000
were awarded to a businessman who was reported
as being "under investigation by the Fraud Squad".
The £217,000 was the total of two awards
by two separate juries against different publications.
But these damages were set aside by the Court of Appeal
and by the House of Lords.
In due course the plaintiff had to accept a much smaller amount.
So, however excessive the jury's original damages,
the process of law prevented them
from being exacted from the newspaper defendants.

In the PQ 17 case, the damages may have seemed high.
CAPTAIN BROOME's £40,000 jury damages
included a punitive element.

If it be argued that the damages
in the PQ 17 case *were* excessive,
my answer is that if I had been on that jury
I would certainly have awarded no less,
and probably much more, against MR DAVID IRVINE
and with no hesitation whatsoever.

---

[1] In 1968 Captain Jack Broome, RN, who had commanded the destroyer escort of the wartime convoy PQ 17, sued for grave libels on him in a book by the controversial historian David Irving. Captain Broome was awarded the enormous sum of £40,000, which included £25,000 "punitive" damages. This was narrowly upheld in the House of Lords but the gallant and unfortunate Captain lost over £13,000 in costs in the protracted appeal process.

I am reinforced in that feeling
by the opinion given to the Faulks Committee
by a distinguished lawyer that £100,000
would not have been excessive in the PQ 17 case.

Then what about the case of KOJAK,
alias MR TELLY SAVALAS?[1]
He was awarded £35,000 for a libel whose sting was
that he had behaved unprofessionally when film-making.
The jury's award of £35,000 was thought
in some quarters[2] to be excessive, though not by the judge,
who later told me that Mr Savalas
was one of the most impressive witnesses
he had ever had before him. And when was there a judge
more moderate and careful in his choice of language
than MR JUSTICE MELFORD STEVENSON?

He may of course have been unduly influenced
by Mr Savalas's innocent and charming smile
when Sir Melford suggested that because
it was a very hot day, wigs could be taken off.
But was £35,000 excessive
for a world star like Savalas?
To him such an amount was chicken-feed.
In my opinion it was no more than he deserved,
bearing in mind that the newspaper could
and should have retracted
at the start, with far less expense to itself.

It is only fair to recall, however,
that the foreman of the jury in the Savalas case
wrote a remarkable letter to *The Times*:

> It is no betrayal of the secrets of the jury room
> to confess that, with the other jurors,
> I entered the Royal Courts of Justice on June 14th

---

[1] Mr Savalas in 1976 sued for an article which had suggested that his nightly carousings while film-making had left him red-eyed and unable to remember his lines.

[2] *The Times* thundered that this sum was "offensively high".

with not the remotest idea what
compensation is paid for anything
except perhaps a dented boot and wing;
haloes are outside our normal terms of reference.
Apparently that is why we were asked.
If that is so, the court had the outcome
it deserved from the appointed procedure.

I am indebted to MR JUSTICE NEILL who is among us tonight
for reminding me of that letter
in his brilliant book *Defamation*,
written jointly with the late COLIN DUNCAN.
But delightful though the foreman's letter was,
its very style and language shows him
to have been more than capable of assessing libel damages.
He says, "Haloes are outside our normal terms of reference" –
that is not the phraseology of a dim-wit.
And though the foreman may have felt ignorant
when the case started, he obviously underestimated the ability
of Mr Justice Melford Stevenson to assist him.

Having said all this in defence of libel juries,
I *would* be in favour of the Court of Appeal
being able to vary a jury award,
but with a limited power to do so.
Would it be reasonable to suggest that the Court of Appeal
should be free to vary an award in those circumstances
in which the Court of Appeal can now order a new trial –
that is to say, when the damages are so large
that no jury properly applying their minds
to the evidence could reasonably have given them?
Or when damages are excessive
in the sense that they exceed even that latitude
which any set of reasonable men could be permitted to indulge?

And I have never been able to understand
why a trial judge should not be able to offer
some guidance by suggesting a range of figures
for the jury's consideration. To some lawyers
and to a reasonable media man that seems perfectly reasonable.
But not to the Faulks Committee.

They wanted the *judge* to fix the damages
after having been advised by the jury
whether the damages should be contemptuous,
nominal, moderate or substantial.
Something, perhaps only instinct,
tells me that it's more sensible for the experienced professional
to help and advise the layman
who then decides, rather than the other way round.

It may be said that our libel law allows the monetary value
of damage to *reputation* to be overestimated.
As to that, I can only cite Shakespeare,
whose authority may be more persuasive than binding.
I make no apology for quoting
these immortal, indeed hackneyed, words.
They are the lines from *Othello*
to be remembered if you ever become so cynical
as to imagine that damage to reputation is not really worth very much:

> Good name in man and woman, dear my lord,
> Is the immediate jewel of their souls.
> Who steals my purse steals trash ...
> But he that filches from me my good name
> Robs me of that which not enriches him,
> And makes me poor indeed.

14 BBC's 60th ANNIVERSARY

July 12th, 1982, Dorchester Hotel. Yet another Variety Club celebration. A banquet in honour of the BBC's 60th anniversary. The speakers were William Whitelaw (Home Secretary), George Howard (BBC Chairman), Frank Muir, Brian Johnston and myself.

I was beginning to make a habit of these BBC anniversary occasions. So I was determined to do something different. Halfway through my speech, I put on a battered Bud Flanagan boater and twirled a silver-topped cane. This created momentary alarm. The audience thought that I was about to sing.

But I did not. I merely referred sadly, and not too seriously, to an ambition of mine, which was not to be achieved for another 19 years, when I sang on the *Des O'Connor Show*, Christmas Eve 1991.

Mr Chief Barker, Home Secretary, my Lords, Ladies and Gentlemen:

I do not want to begin
by creating trouble, because that is not in my nature.

But if I may be absolutely frank
(and when someone says that, you know what to expect),
I really don't know what I'm doing here at all.

Here am I, a small cog in the great machine,
a mere worker on the shop floor,
rubbing shoulders with the powerful
and the rich and the beautiful.
What a gathering this is – politicians, impresarios, tycoons,
mandarins and communicators,
glittering stars of stage, screen and radio.
Not to mention a formidable task force
of senior BBC executives –
several of whom I recognise.
In such a company, I speak with even more than my usual humility.

But I cannot imagine what is expected of me.
Apparently some brilliant planner thought the BBC's health
should be proposed by several people,
each representing a different aspect of broadcasting:

> Mr Brian Johnston for Sport
> Mr Frank Muir for the Creative Arts
> Mr Willie Whitelaw for Politics
> and Mr Robin Day for Light Entertainment.

It is true that I did once appear on a light entertainment programme
called the *Morecambe and Wise Christmas Show.*
I had every reason to believe they were respectable people.
But, do you know, all my jokes were cut out.
Their idea of humour was to beat me
about the head with bottles.
Morecambe and Wise are currently appearing
somewhere on the Thames Embankment.

Yet I am not one to refuse a challenge.
It has always been my secret lifelong dream
to be a music-hall comedian. You know the kind of thing.[1]
Nothing sophisticated.[2]

Alas, it was not to be. Great has been my disappointment.
The BBC has never really understood me.
Do you know, for *years* I've been asking the BBC
to let me have an orchestra.
So that I could dance down some steps
to conduct a stirring item
on the Common Agricultural Policy … or Flexible Rostering.

I did not ask for anything spectacular.
I would have been perfectly happy
with any of the BBC's several orchestras.

As the BBC celebrates 60 glorious years,

---

[1] Here I put a boater on my head and twirled a silver-topped cane.

[2] Here I bent back the brim of the battered boater.

our thoughts, of course, go back
to 1922, the year it all began.

1922 was a year of upheaval.
Historic figures made their exits
and their entrances.
David Lloyd George was thrown out of power.
Horatio Bottomley was sent to prison.
Ian Trethowan[1] was born.

And although *nominally* we are here
to mark the Diamond Jubilee of the BBC,
I congratulate our Director-General most warmly –
indeed I take off my hat to you, Sir Ian –
for having so cleverly arranged on BBC1
this lavish celebration of your own 60th birthday,
which is this very year.

Not even the greatest of your predecessors,
Sir John Reith, ever managed to arrange
for *his* birthday to be celebrated
on the television by the Variety Club of Great Britain.

One of my spare-time activities, Mr Chief Barker,
is to propose the toast of the BBC quite regularly,
every 10 or 20 years or so,
at these enjoyable Variety Club functions.
The last one was in honour of the BBC's *50th* anniversary.
What worries me tonight on the 60th anniversary
is whether I will be proposing the toast of the BBC
for its *80th* anniversary in 2002.

Oh, make no mistake about it,
the Variety Club of Great Britain will still be here.
And *I* have every intention of still being here.

But will the BBC still be here?
Will the BBC, as we have known it,

---

[1] Sir Ian Trethowan, Director-General.

survive beyond the end of this century?

I ask that question because I'm told
we're on the brink of a telecommunications explosion –
an explosion, they say, of volcanic proportions.
Dozens of new TV channels
will be coming into operation through satellites and cables.
Not just four channels but forty perhaps.

It's all very bewildering, not to say alarming.
The Home Secretary, Mr Whitelaw, has been informed.
He is taking a close interest, because he includes broadcasting
among his innumerable responsibilities.
There is no subject of which he has a clearer grasp
than the new multi-channel technology.
Indeed, Mr Whitelaw has already acted with characteristic vigour.
He has set up a committee. And I don't blame him.

How is all this going to work? How will it be paid for?
Who is going to regulate it? Is *anybody* going to regulate it?
Where will it leave the poor old BBC
and its public-service broadcasting, built up over 60 years?
And how will all these new channels and services
develop without plundering the old ones?

That's what Mr Whitelaw may have to decide.
I can only promise the Home Secretary
that if he decides wisely (as I am sure he will)
I shall pay the warmest tribute to his memory
in my speech at the Variety Club's celebration
dinner for the BBC's 80th anniversary in 2002.

Meanwhile, I join in congratulating
the BBC on its 60th anniversary.
May that extraordinary institution,
about which we all love to bellyache,
long continue to deserve
the reputation it enjoys throughout the world
for independence, excellence and fairness.

15 A SPEECH UNSCHEDULED

February 21st, 1985, Dorchester Hotel. This was one of those television awards nights which seem all too frequent. The Royal Television Society gives regular awards, one of which is called the "Judges' Award". This is nothing to do with the law. It is an annual award given by decision of an RTS committee of judges, not by election, but after careful discussion of some special television achievement.

The RTS Judges' Award therefore has considerable prestige in the profession. It was presented to me by Sir Huw Wheldon, President of the RTS, "to mark 30 years of a distinguished and distinctive career in both ITN and BBC TV". The flattering citation with the Award Certificate also described me as "an exemplar of excellence in television reporting", and as having made an "outstanding contribution to broadcast journalism".

The speech I made was not "billed". I do not think it was supposed to be made at all. But it came as welcome light relief for the audience. They had suffered a somewhat pedestrian and earnest evening, with long speeches about the medium, and a procession of worthy award winners for this, that and the other.

Mr President:

Thank you. But I wish to make it clear
that I do not normally attend award ceremonies
of this or any kind.

For one reason, I myself rarely get an award.
I get one, on average, every ten years –
unlike Mr Terry Wogan who gets one at every awards ceremony,
including those where he is presenting the award himself.

Indeed, Mr Wogan got an award two days ago,
and I make no complaint about that

except that the programme extract
which was shown to illustrate Mr Wogan's talent
consisted solely of *me* being interviewed by *him*,
and there was precious little to be heard of *him*.

Another good reason for avoiding award ceremonies
is the extraordinary behaviour of many award winners.
At all other times they are articulate and self-assertive people.
Yet when they receive an award, they stutter and mutter
about not really deserving the award,
or that all the credit is due to other people.

Perhaps, like me, you have longed for the moment
when some award winner will simply say,
"I accept this award with the utmost enthusiasm —
indeed, I think it is long overdue."
Only my natural humility prevents me
from saying anything like that tonight.
Do sit down, Sir Huw.[1]

As to the professional colleagues
I have had to work w... I've worked with
during the last 30 years,
you will be glad to know
that I do not propose to thank them all by name.

I will simply congratulate them all
on having had the inestimable good fortune
to work with me. Several of them are here tonight
among the imposing ranks of senior BBC executives
(many of whom I recognise)
and among the distinguished ITV contingent.
Oh yes, all human life is here.

As I look around, I see many old friends. But now
they are Managing Director of this, Controller of that,
Chief Executive of the other ...
Here they are in all their power and their glory.

[1] This to Sir Huw Wheldon, who had remained standing on the mistaken assumption that I was not going to make a speech.

When I think of Brian Wenham, Jeremy Isaacs and Paul Fox,
I sometimes feel that television is virtually
all run by former Editors of *Panorama*
to whom I have given varying degrees of trouble.

Sir Huw, I accept this award with gratitude.
But I hope that the gifted Editor of *Question Time*,
Barbara Maxwell, will not regard it as a hint,
a hint that enough is enough.

I happen to think that this award marks a very important moment.
Because it shows, thank God, that the cult of youth is over.
This is the time of the Golden Oldies.
Sir Huw, I do not refer only to myself.
Others who are still with us come to mind:

I would like to mention one name on this occasion. He is not here.
He gave me my first job in television
at the founding of ITN in 1955.
Aidan Crawley recently recovered from a very serious accident.
I owe him a great debt. And he is a lovely man,
and I thank him very much.

Sir Huw: it is a great honour to be in your presence.
You are indeed the Monarch of the Medium.
Landseer[1] should have painted your picture.
Thank you very much indeed. Goodnight.

[1] Featured in Wheldon's TV series on royal paintings at Balmoral, etc.

MINISTERIAL WHITEBAIT

October 21st, 1985, Trafalgar Tavern, Greenwich. The Saints and Sinners' Club of London has long been established for dining and lunching and for raising funds for charities. Its membership is limited to 100, who are a raffish mixture of entertainment stars, eminent politicians, sportsmen and other celebrities – all male. At their formal functions, those who regard themselves as Saints wear white carnations, and the Sinners red.

The speeches made at the Saints and Sinners' functions are traditionally none too serious. The members and their guests are usually in a pleasantly convivial state.

In 1985 I was a guest at two of their functions. The first was at their "Ministerial Whitebait Dinner". This was held at Greenwich. The Speaker and several of Mrs Thatcher's Cabinet – Chancellor Nigel Lawson and Home Secretary Douglas Hurd, for instance – were among the guest speakers, as was I.

Most of the Saints and Sinners and their Right Honourable guests had travelled to Greenwich by boat from Westminster pier, the tradition being to sample the first whitebait of the season.

Each of the 11 or so speakers was asked to speak for not more than one-and-a-half minutes. My speech came last. It overran a little because of the laughter, so that was all right.

Mr Chairman, Mr Speaker, Your Excellency,
Lords, Ladies and Gentlemen:

I would prefer not to begin by creating trouble,
because that is not in my nature.
I have an overwhelming sense of being redundant.
To be one of 11 speakers is bad enough.
But I am instructed to speak "in a light-hearted vein"
for one-and-a-half minutes.
There is hardly any point in coming here.

But 30 years in television
have accustomed me to the ruthless discipline of time.
On one occasion I was a guest commentator
in Washington, DC, at the inauguration of a President.
During the rehearsal,
the director called down from the control room,
"At this point in the parade, Robin,
I want you and Ed and Mort
[Ed and Mort were the other two commentators]
to throw it around between the three of you –
for 30 seconds."

May I now begin my speech,
which has already overrun its allotted time?

Before this brilliant and imposing audience
of Cabinet Ministers, parliamentarians and other entertainers,
I speak with even more than my usual humility.

Because I, alas, am not one of those broadcasters
who bring happiness into your hearts
or laughter into your homes.
I am a messenger of misery, a herald of conflict and gloom.

Would that it were not so.
How wonderful to be one of those popular
and celebrated interviewers,
whose dreadf… delightful chat-shows
make them stars of the entertainment world.
How wonderful to have the gift
of being able to make your guests
seem almost as beautiful and celebrated as yourself.

How wonderful to be Terry Wogan:
not merely because of his money,
though one would take that into account –
a numbered Swiss account.
Look at the kind of people
whose knees Wogan can stroke –
Joan Collins and Boy George.
Look at me. I count myself lucky to sit between

Eric Heffer and Sir Geoffrey H...
Howe wonderful to be David Frost.
Now there's a unique figure.
He's the only human being who actually looks
like a Scotland Yard Identikit picture.

How wonderful to be Sir Alastair Burnet,
whom I used to know when he was just an ordinary fellow,
before he was playing the Palace.

I suffer from professional nightmares.
The latest one being that I am at No. 10
to interview the Prime Minister.
I hear myself beginning, "Prime Minister,
what is your answer to my first question?"

I was once preparing to interview a Prime Minister,
whose name at the moment eludes me.
I sought the advice of an old
and famous High Court judge as to how to start.
I should explain that the then Prime Minister
was not at the height of his political reputation.
The old judge pondered. Eventually he said,
"You should begin the interview like this:
'Prime Minister, does the word *shame* mean anything to you?'"

I am slowly recovering my health.
I have just attended the four party conferences.
As always, the most significant comments
were not made in public for the television cameras.

At the Labour Party conference in Bournemouth,
for example, one elderly Welsh delegate was heard to say
after one of Mr Kinnock's two brilliant speeches,
"*Very* dangerous. A very dangerous speech indeed.
A few more speeches like that and we could be in power."

A kindly viewer wrote to me the other day to warn,
"You must realise you are now in the departure lounge of life."
Happily the next Sinners' flight has been a little delayed.

17 HECKLED BY THE PRIME MINISTER

December 6th, 1985, Savoy Hotel. My one-and-a-half minutes at the Ministerial Whitebait Dinner led to another invitation. I was asked to speak at the Saints and Sinners' Christmas Lunch that December. Margaret Thatcher was the other guest speaker. The Prime Minister was the only woman present.

So these occasions, though both run by the Saints and Sinners, were very different. The Whitebait Dinner at Greenwich was an uproarious party. The Christmas Lunch at the Savoy with the Prime Minister present and speaking was more decorous.

The Prime Minister spoke first. Then it was my turn.

Mr President, Mr Chairman, Prime Minister,
Gentlemen, Saints, Sinners and those
who are not arrogant enough to be the former,
or not honest enough to be the latter:

At this late hour, I feel distinctly surplus – indeed, redundant.

What on earth, Mr Chairman, did you have in mind
when you planned this feast of oratory?
Perhaps in your innocence you saw me
as the savoury soufflé to follow the cabinet pudding?
Or as I would put it more gallantly,
the frivolous trifle to follow the main dish?[1]

But on such a festive occasion as this,
I have an overwhelming sense of being wholly unsuitable.
I, alas, am not one of those broadcasters who bring happiness
into your hearts or laughter into your homes.
Even the programme in which I appear

---

[1] The PM smiled her wintry appreciation.

will be taken off by Michael Grade over the Christmas holiday period
because I, like Rambo,
am not fit for family festive viewing.

But I must count my blessings.
I get up each morning with a smile –
as soon as I have checked
that I am not in the *Times* obituary.

I think, "What a wonderful place to live."
Inflation is being curbed.
A gentleman can still buy a decent bottle of claret
for only £105,000.[1]

And what a pleasure to be here today,
in the presence of the Prime Minister, bishops,
sundry parliamentarians
and other stars of the entertainment world.

Whenever I think of the Prime Minister
(and she will be happy to know
she is very often in my thoughts)
I think of that memorable general election year, 1959.
That was a significant year in British political history.
It was the year that Margaret Thatcher
succeeded in entering Parliament,
and the year that I *failed* to enter Parliament.
By such quirks of the popular will
is the destiny of great nations decided.

But just suppose – and I see this query
forming in your mischievous minds –
"Suppose it had been the other way round?"
A very interesting question.
But lead me not into temptation.

I took that defeat in 1959 philosophically.
I was brought up on the maxim "Trust the People",

---

[1] A bargain reported in the press that week.

and in the circumstances I had little option but so to do.
I took the 1959 result like a man,
and so (one might say) did Mrs Thatcher.

[*Prime Minister very audibly heckles:*
"I did much better than that."]

If I may continue, Mr Chairman.
Nowadays I maintain a respectful friendship
with my distinguished contemporaries
who have succeeded where I failed.
I greet them with warmth and affection,
however big a hash they may be making of it.

My friends in the Cabinet always take it remarkably well
when I give them a cordial salutation:
"Still clinging to office, I see."
They laugh, because they think I am joking.

May I say one serious thing to the Prime Minister today?
I say it with the greatest respect.
So you can guess what may be coming.

She has recently been a disappointment to me.
I am not referring to her conduct of Government policy
or to her leadership of the nation.
I respectfully leave such criticism
to my eminent contemporaries, such as the Earl of Stockton,[1]
not to mention all those Marxist bishops.
Incidentally when Lord Stockton came to that historic dinner
at No. 10 the other night, how thoughtful of the Prime Minister
to have kept some of the family silver for him to eat off.

No, what disappointed me
was the Prime Minister's vote against an experiment
in televising the House of Commons.
I do not expect her to change her mind
in the next two minutes.

[1] The former Prime Minister, Harold Macmillan.

I ask only one question: does it make sense
for the nation's prime forum of debate
to shut itself off
from the prime medium of mass communication?

Mr Chairman, you and your fellow self-appointed Saints
and self-confessed Sinners
are hospitable and charitable, and in many cases fairly respectable.
The Saints and Sinners have one great virtue in common:
they know where they are going
when the time comes.

In the meantime, I have the honour
to ask my fellow guests, including the Prime Minister,
to drink the health of the Saints and Sinners.

18 THE GOLDEN JUBILEE OF TELEVISION

November 1st, 1986, Grosvenor House. This was the Royal Television Society's Golden Ball, given to mark the Golden Jubilee of Television. The first public television service had been started by the BBC in November 1936.

The President of the RTS, Paul Fox, invited me to speak. I appear to have been responding to a toast.

The audience was several hundred people from the world of television, both ITV and the BBC. One guest at the top table attracted much attention. This was Mr Marmaduke Hussey, whose appointment as the new Chairman of the BBC had come as a surprise.

It was a time of mounting tension between the BBC and Tory ministers. According to Kenneth Rose, writing in the *Sunday Telegraph*'s Albany column, "Sir Robin's final words contrasted sharply with the self-congratulatory mood of his BBC colleagues. His last robust sentence was as welcome as a ham sandwich in a synagogue."

Mr President:

I would prefer not to begin
by creating trouble (because that is not in my nature)
but I really don't understand
why I have been invited to open the cabaret
on this festive occasion.
I am a messenger of misery,
a herald of conflict and gloom.

Would that it were not so.
Would that I could be reincarnated.
For example, how wonderful to be Terry Wogan:
not merely because of the money he makes,

though one would take that into account –
a numbered Swiss account.

How wonderful to be Mr Wogan, who sits between
Joan Collins and Gary Glitter.
I'm lucky to sit between Edwina Currie and Sir Geoffrey
Howe wonderful – how much more wonderful –
to be Sir Alastair Burnet.
He is now preparing the first ever,
hour long, in depth, no holds barred interview
with HRH Prince William
in a new Royal soap series called *Bath-time with Burnet*.

How wonderful, instead of being an old stager,
to be a new star –
Mr Robert Kilroy-Silk for example.
He has achieved the ultimate.
He has become a heart-throb, a sex-symbol,
and the housewives' choice –
without ever having yet appeared
on his TV programme at all!
If he takes my advice, Mr Kilroy-Silk will quit TV while he's at the top,
and do something else – like go into Parliament.[1]

But to be fair, Mr Kilroy-Silk has a problem.
He is quoted as saying,
"People think I am just a pretty face.
And because I am so good-looking,
they think there can't be much between my ears.
It is a genuine handicap."
Some of us, Mr President, know exactly how he feels.

Mr President: to honour the pioneers of 50 years ago,
the Royal Television Society has assembled here
a glittering company: producers, performers,
engineers, designers, tycoons,
trade union leaders, impresarios, parliamentarians –
and one Duke (a warm welcome to Mr Hussey,

[1] Kilroy-Silk had just left Parliament, amid much advance publicity, for his new career on TV.

and I congratulate him on recovering so quickly
from the shock of his appointment),[1]
along with a task force of senior BBC executives,
several of whom I recognise.

I don't have much experience of Golden Balls.
But you obviously can't have a Golden Ball
without a Golden Oldie.
I have appeared on television
for most of these 50 years —
for over three-fifths of them, anyway.

But every 10 or 20 years or so,
I am wheeled out to speak at one of these happy events.
No one enjoys more than I the beguiling nostalgia
and the gross flattery of these occasions.
But they often seem to be overshadowed
by some television crisis,
confrontation, clash, conspiracy or cock-up,
which is usually accompanied
by a newspaper chorus of "heads must roll".

So if one is making a speech, as I usually am,
one has to tread very carefully, as I usually do.

Talking of "heads rolling",
a former television executive wrote to the press
to explain that in *his* time,
"heads must roll" always turned out
to mean "*assistant* heads must roll".

This is a BBC anniversary,
but it is a Royal Television Society party,
presided over by you,[2] Sir,
who are Managing Director
of Yorkshire Television and Chairman of Independent Television News.

---

[1] Marmaduke Hussey, newly appointed Chairman of the BBC, known as Duke or Dukey.

[2] Sir Paul Fox, CBE, who rejoined the BBC as Managing Director of TV in 1988.

I have followed your career with admiration
ever since you were Editor of *Panorama*.
That was in those dear days beyond recall,
when *Panorama* was a magazine programme
called *The Window on the World*.
And you were known as Five Item Fox.
You found me then a perpetual nuisance.
Week after week I urged you
to show flair, nerve and imagination.
And you did, quite often.

As I look at the ITN table
(I can see which it is because of the haloes they are all wearing).[1]
I see my old friend and former editor,
Sir Geoffrey Cox, architect of *News at Ten,*
whose devotion to impartiality and balance is legendary.
So much so, that the producer of an ITN documentary on the Holy
    Land
asked him if he was expected to give equal time to Pontius Pilate.

The event we are celebrating tonight,
the birth of BBC Television,
took place in a very different world from today.
1936 was halfway between the depression and the war.
The Prime Minister was Mr Stanley Baldwin.
A new monarch, Edward VIII, was on the throne.
But not for much longer.
Abdication was only a few weeks away.
The cockney boys were soon to be on the streets
with their Christmas carol for 1936:

    Hark the herald angels sing
    Mrs Simpson's pinched our King.

1936 was the year that war became inevitable.
It was the age of appeasement.
Herr Hitler was goose-stepping in Berlin
(and if you think I'm going to do my impersonation,
you're going to be disappointed).[1]

---

[1] ITN, in contrast to BBC News, had lately won praise from the Thatcher government.

The very night the BBC TV Service was inaugurated,
Winston Churchill was warning
in a speech at the Savoy Hotel,
"A strong Britain means the peace of the world.
A weak Britain opens the door to disaster."
Nobody paid much attention.

And nobody paid very much attention
to the inauguration of the BBC,
the world's first public television service.

The evening of November 2nd, 1936
wasn't exactly a mass-audience occasion.
Even by the end of that year,
only 280 television sets had been sold.

Within a month, Sir John Reith admitted
that he had been much more impressed by television
than he had expected.

The BBC Controller of Public Relations
said he felt no doubt about the popular appeal
of the new TV Service,
particularly "among the less educated".

Who knows what will happen to television
in the next half-century?
Will there still be a BBC or an ITV?

Will we have ascended into the heaven
of deregulated multiplicity of choice,
a free market in TV channels,
"electronic publishing"
as it is called,
with TV as free and unbridled
as books, magazines and newspapers?

Will we look back on our present system

---

[1] A risky reference to a Tory MP's libel action against the BBC.

of regulated, licensed public service broadcasting
as monstrously illiberal,
just as we now condemn the licensing
and censorship of printing,
against which Milton fought in the 17th century?

Your guess, Mr President, is as good as mine.
In fact, your guess is much better than mine.
For you are President of the Royal Television Society.
I am merely the man on the Clapham Omnibus.
I am but a humble worker on the shop floor
of what your distinguished predecessor, Sir Huw Wheldon,
used to call "the great television factory".

And we who are working there hope to soldier
on with such independence and freedom
as we enjoy under the present system.

This great celebration happens to come at a worrying time.
"The Corporation," according to *The Times*,
"has Norman Tebbit's stiletto at its throat."
Some stiletto! Some throat!

Politicians of all parties have a right
to protest, to complain, and have always done so,
especially in the run-up to a general election.

But politicians of all parties
know that they have a duty
to uphold our independence and not to undermine it.
We in television have a corresponding duty
to be truthful, fair and responsible,
otherwise our independence will be in danger.

In that spirit, I have great pleasure
in responding to your toast.

19 MY SKIRMISH WITH CARDIAC SURGERY

December 11th, 1988, Gleneagles Hotel, Scotland. I had been asked by a professor in Glasgow to talk to a symposium of doctors about my multiple heart bypass operation. This had been done three years previously, in 1985, and repaired in 1986.

I was inclined not to accept this invitation, as I lacked the clinical knowledge to address an international symposium of doctors about cardiology.

These doubts and objections were brushed aside. I accepted the force of the professor's argument, that many of the doctors in my audience would have had little or no direct experience of patients who had had heart bypass operations, which were then not so common as now. And a weekend at Gleneagles, one of the most luxurious and beautifully situated hotels in the world, would be a pleasant change, even in December, from London.

Also, uniquely in my speech-making experience, there was a fee, though this was relatively modest and not decisive.

I was to give the keynote address of the symposium. My talk came within minutes of the doctors checking in at the hotel. Late arrivals took their seats as I was speaking.

So I had to warm up my cold audience of doctors. How much they got out of it I could not be sure. But a year or so later, Professor Shepherd wrote again, asking me to repeat my keynote address at another symposium of the same kind.

I politely declined with thanks. Fee or no fee, I wanted to forget the operation, not to keep on reliving it, not to become an exhibit.

Mr Chairman, Ladies and Gentlemen:

I am bound to say that I do not feel
a very suitable person to deliver this keynote address
in the citadel of cardiac disease –
I refer not to Gleneagles but to Scotland.

Alas, I am totally unlearned and undistinguished.
I failed in two professions,
first the Bar and then Politics,
and have only just managed to make do
in a much less significant occupation, namely television.

So standing before this professional audience
of cardiologists and other experienced practitioners,
I speak with even more than my usual humility.[1]

I speak on the subject of your symposium
tonight with almost complete ignorance.
I am not a doctor or a surgeon.
Indeed for *most* of my life, I am happy to say,
I have had nothing whatsoever to do
with the medical profession.
Except, of course, when visiting my unfortunate GPs.
One of my GPs committed suicide.
Another broke his neck sleepwalking.

But don't misunderstand me. Many of my best friends
are members of the medical profession.

Moreover, I have never had a heart attack.
Nor do I take any special interest
in health matters. I simply consider myself lucky to be alive
and to have reached the age of 65.
I have spent most of my adult life
suffering from chronic obesity,
and a heavy addiction to smoking
until six years ago, a lamentable lack of exercise,

---

[1] For once, this stock line of mine was all too sincere.

and the intolerable stress and strain
and stopwatch timing of television.
Not to mention indulging in scrambled eggs for breakfast,
as in Glasgow this morning.

Despite these regrettable facts,
my life until about the age of 60
was virtually doctor-free.
Because of those regrettable facts
I have, since about the age of 60,
been in more or less daily communication
with the medical profession.

So who am I to give this keynote address?
Well, the original invitation to me
from Professor Shepherd read as follows:

> Your coronary bypass surgery has been
> a hot topic of conversation in the
> medical profession, particularly in
> the light of a recent article in the
> *Sunday Times*.

To have become a "hot topic of conversation"
among doctors is indeed a sign of celebrity,
but I beg leave to doubt if any doctors,
other than my own, even considered my experience
of bypass surgery – if indeed they were aware of it.

Earlier this year, I telephoned Professor Shepherd
to protest that I was inadequate for this keynote address.
"Don't you want some sort of expert?" I said.
"But you *are* an expert," he said. "You've had this operation."
"But so has practically everyone else that I know.
In any case, I know nothing about the operation.
I was under an anaesthetic at the time."

Professor Shepherd replied, "But you know much more about it
than most of your audience."

Such was the professor's beguiling sense of humour
that I agreed to deliver this keynote address.
The invitation described it as "highlighting my skirmish

with surgical cardiology", of which, as he said, I am a survivor.
So far.

Then I began to suspect that Professor Shepherd
did not really expect me to contribute seriously,
but wanted me to be a comic opening turn to your proceedings –
a sort of cardiac cabaret.
He even went so far as to suggest (and I quote)
that "a *light-hearted* approach would be welcome".
In other word a delicate hors d'oeuvre,
a frivolous soufflé before the Gleneagles feast with a rich, heavy menu.

Light-hearted approach? From me?
I'm afraid I have to disappoint you.
No, I am merely an elderly political reporter
who is now, as a viewer wrote
the other day, "in the departure lounge of life".

While I await my flight, which has fortunately been delayed,
I cannot promise to be entertaining or instructive.
But I can at least give you one layman's account
of his experience of cardiac surgery,
of what is known as a coronary bypass operation.
And I can offer you some thought and reflections
which may be of general relevance,
even though the case of every vict… patient is different.

It so happens that I have been able to discuss the bypass operation
with a lot of other people who have had it.
Because anyone who has had a coronary bypass
belongs to a club –
a club admittedly getting less exclusive as it gets more fashionable.
And the members get a certain macabre pleasure
out of sharing their experiences.
And if one happens to be notorious from television appearances,
one is liable to attract (or at least I did)
many conversations and communications
about this particular operation.
So I have often discussed the operation and its effects,
good or bad, with others who have also had it.

Among the great and the good
with whom I have compared notes in conversation

or correspondence have been Lord Chancellor Havers,
John Cole (Political Editor of the BBC),
Lord Murray of Epping Forest (alias Len Murray of the TUC),
Anthony Sampson (the author),
Lord McAlpine (Treasurer of the Tory Party),
Derek Gladwin of the Municipal Workers' Union,
Dr Henry Kissinger, and John Stonehouse, MP.
All of them have had the operation,
not to mention several TV viewers previously unknown to me.

I corresponded with the late John Stonehouse
who had had his bypass while serving his prison sentence.
Mr Stonehouse wrote to me
when I had my operation, to express the hope
that I would have better company
for my convalescence than he had.
His companions, he said, included Peter Sutcliffe,
the Yorkshire Ripper, and Ian Brady, the Moors Murderer.

There is something about this extraordinary operation
which creates a curious camaraderie between those who have it.

I was once on a train from Bournemouth,
hiding behind my copy of *The Times*,
when a distinguished-looking gentleman came into the compartment
and began reading *his* copy of *The Times*.
Then he began to eye me over the top of his paper.
"Am I right in thinking," he said,
"that we have had the same operation?"

He was a general, just retired from a top Army post.[1]
Immediately we, who were complete strangers,
were as old friends,
reminiscing with gruesome enthusiasm,
and proudly showing each other our war wounds
and recalling, what Professor Shepherd would call,
our "skirmishes with surgical cardiology".

Indeed, anyone passing down the corridor of that train

---

[1] General Sir Richard Worsley, GCB, OBE.

who had happened to peer into that first-class compartment
would have seen the remarkable sight
of two apparently respectable gentlemen
excitedly rolling up their trousers
and pointing admiringly at each other's bare legs,
which the surgeon's knife had slashed
to get the veins needed for the bypass.

One of the special characteristics of this branch of surgery
is that the patient does carry about
visible and bodily evidence of his treatment,
evidence which can be displayed
at the swimming pool or in the bedroom.
Apart from the scar down the front of his chest,
he has long scars on his legs, in my case on both legs –
on the left leg running from ankle to groin.

To quote the article by the *Sunday Times* medical correspondent,
which became, apparently, a talking point in medical circles:
"The procedure is a tribute to modern surgical skill.
Patients are cut open almost from neck to abdomen" –
I would say from neck to ankle –
"and veins from the leg are grafted on
to improve the heart's blood supply."

I was myself quoted in this *Sunday Times* article
as saying, "I felt like an old gentleman cut to pieces."
That is not accurate. I did *not* say,
"I felt like an old gentleman cut to pieces."
I said, "I *am* an old gentleman cut to pieces!"

Now, the question of interest is whether the operation is,
on balance, a good idea or not.

According to the *Sunday Times* medical correspondent
there was no clear-cut evidence of prolonged life,
although these trials did suggest a life-saving effect
in certain severely diseased patients.

As you know, the number of such operations
has increased dramatically during the last ten years,
from just over 3,000 in the UK in 1978

to nearly 12,000 in 1985.
And estimates for more recent years suggest
that the number here
will have quintupled during the last ten years.

I was told (this was in '85) that the heart bypass operation
had become in the USA
the second most common major operation.

What has been the effect in my case? Firstly, I am still alive.
Two questions arise from *that statement.*
Would I now be dead but for the operation?
Am I more alive than I would have been?
In other words, has my health improved?

To answer the first of these questions,
I can only tell you what my cardiologist told me
when the operation was first mooted.
He said, "Your chances of having a major heart attack
within five years will be 5 per cent,
as opposed to 50 per cent if you don't have the operation."

So I had the operation, in March 1985.
The facts in my case are doubtless similar
to many in your experience. I was then aged 61.
I had not had a heart attack,
but complained to my doctor
of slight pains in the chest when walking.

I was passed to a cardiologist
who subjected me to cardiac catheterisation,
which produced an angiogram.
This gave a remarkable picture
of my arteries and their blockages.

When the angiogram picture was projected for my edification
on to the wall of my surgeon's consulting room
I thought it looked like a map of the London Underground.
What I thought were the stations were blockages.

In due course, I was operated on –
to quote the language of my consultant cardiothoracic surgeon[1] –

to revascularise *six* of my coronary arteries.
(That rather impressed Dr Henry Kissinger,
who had only three arteries revascularised.)

Now I come to the more interesting question.
Am I more alive now than I would have been?
Has the quality of my life, on balance, improved?
Is my health and well-being better now
than it would have been but for the operation?

The honest answer is in some ways "yes"
(I am still alive) and in some ways "no".
I certainly felt in better health
in the year or so following the operation.
My appetite became even bigger and I felt more vigorous.
But the left leg, from which most of the vein for grafting
was taken, remains uncomfortably swollen,
especially at the ankle.

In the last two years I have felt increasingly tired
and less inclined to take the vigorous daily exercise
which I was recommended.
And I have experienced a number of other problems.
But these may be due as much to natural senility
as to the effects of the six bypasses.

I was rather unlucky in one respect.
Although from the cardiovascular point of view
my multiple bypass operation was very successful,
there was what I can only describe
as a mechanical failure – or metal fatigue.
This condition was discovered not by the vigilance
or expert scrutiny of my cardiologist,
but by a lady of my acquaintance who is not a doctor.

This lady happened to be resting her head on my chest.
I forget why – it need not concern you –
I think we were discussing
the public sector borrowing requirement,
or nuclear disarmament, or something.

---

[1]Mr Gareth Rees, MS, FRCP. FRCS.

Anyway, she suddenly said to me, "You're clicking."
I said (somewhat put out), "But I do not click.
I have never clicked in my life."
She replied, "If you don't believe me,
go and see your doctor."

So I went to see my cardiologist,
who listened in on his stethoscope and confirmed that I clicked,
or, as he phrased it to me,
"You have a disunited or mobile sternum."

The cardiologist sent me back to the surgeon.
The surgeon advised me to have
another operation to reunite my sternum.
I'm not sure why my sternum had become disunited.
Presumably it was because the steel sutures either
were not strong enough or were not numerous enough.
Or perhaps I did too much exertion too soon.
Anyway, a year after the first operation,
I had to be opened up again and wired up again.

That was an experience more unpleasant than the first,
involving another nine-day stay in hospital.
Letters from unknown viewers who had
read about my second operation
indicated that their sternums are liable to disunite.

One viewer wrote to cheer me up
by saying his sternum had had to be reunited
three times after his bypass operation.
His family had suggested
that his sternum should have a zip fastener.

For me, that second operation came as a strain and a setback.
But the following year my surgeon reported
that I had a stable and well-healed sternum.
Certainly I have had no further complaints about clicking.

I would ask one or two questions about post-operative care.
Is it satisfactory for patients
who have had this massive operation
simply to be sent home after a week in hospital?

Of course, they are given advice, as I was,
on what to do and what not to do
in the months following the operation.
But do they not need a period or programme
of rehabilitation,
if not in hospital at least in some centre for rehabilitation?

An American described to me in some detail
his post-operative rehabilitation programme,
which included regular visits to a centre for appropriate exercise.
Nothing of that kind was prescribed or suggested for me,
only that I should walk regularly, and keep to a sensible diet.

Also, the swift discharge from hospital to one's home
may not be best for the patient.
I am fairly certain that one reason
why my sternum became disunited
following my operation was that
I had no alternative but to exert myself
in ways which I was advised not to,
for example carrying luggage, opening iron lift-gates,
moving heavy objects, etc.

What else can I usefully tell you?

Only that my own life is abundant proof,
if proof is needed, that prevention
would have been better than cure,
and better than bypass surgery.

The only achievement in which I can take pride
is that I had stopped smoking completely on March 27th, 1982.
And, curiously enough, I feel no urge to resume, no deprivation.

You see before you a sinner not a saint.
But you will be glad to know
that I do not sin against the 11th commandment,
which the Almighty handed down when he created television:
"Thou shalt not exceed thy allotted time."

20 LUNCH TO LAUNCH MY MEMOIRS

November 1st, 1989, Grosvenor House Hotel. Foyle's Literary Luncheons are a regular, time-honoured feature of the London publishing scene. Miss Christina Foyle, owner of the world-famous bookshop, long ago created a tradition with her luncheons for celebrated authors and their books. In the huge dining-room of a grand hotel are scores of people who have bought tickets for the lunch. Most of them will also buy an autographed copy of the book for which the luncheon is held. Part of the fun for them is a close look at the celebrities whom Miss Foyle invites to be guests of honour at the long top table.

This Foyle's luncheon was for my memoirs, *Grand Inquisitor*. The guests of honour included Lord Callaghan of Cardiff, Lord Grimond, Roy Hattersley, Sir Geoffrey Cox, Ludovic Kennedy and his wife Moira Shearer, Lord Goodman, Lord Weidenfeld (my publisher) and Christopher Chataway.

At my request, the lunch was presided over by Lord Hailsham of St Marylebone, KG, CH, PC, FRS, aged 83. He was in splendidly eloquent form so much so that the first part of my speech was about him, not my memoirs.

My Lord Chairman:

You do me great honour by presiding at this session.
You have been a charismatic, eloquent and controversial figure
in our public life for over half a century.
You have been the most intellectually brilliant
and the most colourful Lord Chancellor
since the days of the great F E Smith.

You have been a great parliamentarian
on both the red and the green benches.
On radio and television

you are a magnificent broadcaster
who has never given a dull broadcast in his life.
In that connection I refer to page 183 in my book.
I take great pleasure there
in recording one momentous and memorable interview with you
in the small hours of general election results night, 1966.
Dr Robert McKenzie's swingometer
quite clearly showed a Wilson landslide.
Into the studio came Mr Quintin Hogg, as you then were.
The interviewer began (and I quote from the transcript):

> Mr Hogg, will you now take a back seat
> in the Tory Party after this Labour victory?
> *Answer:* I shall play as big a part as God will allow me.
> *Question:* And how big a part do you think God will allow you
>   to play?
> *Answer:* You will have to ask him.
> *[I should explain that it was 3.30 in the morning.]*
> *Question:* I don't think he's on our list of people that we interview.
> *Answer:* No, you will have to pay him too big a fee.

I am delighted not only by your chairmanship,
but by the presence here
of some good friends of mine who are at this table.
First, Sir Geoffrey Cox, who was Editor of ITN
just after my start in television in the mid '50s.
He became a great television journalist
and was the architect of *News at Ten*.
Secondly, Paul Fox, Managing Director of BBC Television
and President of the Royal Television Society.
I spotted him as a BBC executive of flair and imagination,
particularly if he agreed with my advice,
when he was Editor of *Panorama*.

I am also delighted to see on this table
elder statesmen, rising stars of the Westminster stage,
media personalities of one kind or another,
many of whom are mentioned in my book
with varying degrees of respect.
In the presence of such an impressive gathering
of orators and media stars

you will understand, my Lord Chairman,
that I speak this afternoon with even more than my usual humility.

This autumn is a bad time to publish memoirs.
There has been a flood of autobiographical works.
There has been David Steel, Denis Healey,
 and Tony Benn's *Diaries*, Volume 3.
They are all competing with my humble volume.
And we must not forget my old and dear friend Ludovic Kennedy,
whose own memoirs have done disappointingly well.

My memoirs are simply those
of an elderly political reporter, a very dull dog indeed.
Unlike other memoirs, whose name I will not mention,
there are no intimate, scandalous revelations,
and there are no confessions.
I write as an extinct volcano.
Only the other day I received a letter from a viewer saying,
"Now that you have reached the departure lounge of life ..."
Happily, my plane has been delayed
to enable me to attend this Foyle's Luncheon.

I see that Mr Gerald Kaufman, MP, kindly referred
in the *Sunday Times* to "this ebullient yet endearing volume".
Ladies and Gentlemen, I have been
in the television business for 35 years,
laboriously building a reputation as aggressive,
acerbic, insulting and unpleasant
to practically everybody on the most impartial basis.
And now I end up by being described as "endearing".
How big a failure can you be?

You will be glad to know that this book is not about me alone.
It deals with television as a medium.
I discuss the most difficult question
that broadcasters have had to face
since television was invented.
In a free society which has a tradition
of independence in broadcasting,
how do you prevent television from becoming an ally of terrorism?
I do not think we have found the answer to that problem yet.

I also mention how, for over 30 years,
I have advocated the case for televising Parliament.
Parliament now is about to be televised.
What no commentator has appreciated
is that this historic change is happening
at a time of upheaval in our political life.

The cameras are going into the Commons' chamber
at the moment when the political landscape appears to be changing.
The question on everyone's lips is:
is the ascendancy of Margaret Thatcher at an end?
We do not know. We shall see.[1]

The confrontation on television, from the House of Commons,
seen in our homes, will have an extraordinary effect.
I cannot say what that effect will be.
We shall see how the experiment works out.
It is a development of immense importance
and it comes at a fascinating political time.

Ladies and Gentlemen, in these memoirs of mine
you will find reminiscences; you will find reflections;
there is a mixture of all these in the book. I thank you for listening.

[1] We did indeed see. Margaret Thatcher was forced from power only one year later.

21 TED'S 40TH

February 21st, 1990, Savoy Hotel. This was the most extraordinary, and at the same time enjoyable, lunchtime celebration I have ever attended. It was held in honour of Ted Heath's 40th anniversary as a Member of Parliament. He had first been elected in February 1950.

The atmosphere in the Savoy Hotel was electric. This was because the Prime Minister, Margaret Thatcher, was coming to this lunch in honour of Ted Heath. Would they speak to each other? (They did.) Would they shake hands? (They did.) Would she make a speech? (She did not.)

The audience was several hundred politicians and public figures, not all Conservatives, who had been colleagues or friends or officials during Ted Heath's long career as parliamentarian and Prime Minister.

The benign and neutral chairman was Lord Home of the Hirsel.[1] He sat between Margaret Thatcher and Ted Heath.

Various names had been given to me of those who were expected to make speeches. In the end, apart from the chairman the list boiled down to Ted Heath, Lord (Jim) Prior and myself.

The Archbishop of Canterbury, Dr Runcie, said grace. For this occasion, he had composed a special grace. He had taken great trouble, Dr Runcie told me, to see that it was "carefully balanced". Between what, or whom, I wondered, without asking the question aloud.

Such was the atmosphere and the company. No speech-maker had a more responsive audience than I did that day.

[1] Who, as Sir Alec Douglas-Home, had been Prime Minister for a year, 1963–64.

Lord Home, Prime Minister,
My Lords, Ladies and Gentlemen:

I have an overwhelming sense
of being redundant and out of place.

Here am I, amid this august gathering of Church and State,
of the Great and the Good, of the Wet and the Dry.

Everyone is here. Two archbishops, the Prime Minister herself,
former Prime Ministers,
future Prime Ministers
(I can see at least six of those),
not to mention innumerable grandees and golden oldies.

Before such an audience, I speak
with even more than my usual humility.
Why am I here?
I've never been a parliamentarian.
Nor a member of the Tory Party.
Nor a card-carrying European.
Nor have I ever conducted an orchestra.

I can only assume I've been asked to speak
as a member of what Mr Bernard Ingham[1] recently called
"that raddled, disease-racked body, the media".

It has been my good fortune and privilege
to cross swords with Ted Heath
on television at many critical moments
in his long parliamentary career,
at moments of victory and triumph,
at moments of defeat and frustration.

Those interviews were not always appreciated by his supporters,
but Ted never complained or objected.
And he never seemed to bear me the slightest ill-will.
Until one day which I remember well.

---

[1] Mrs Thatcher's pugnacious Press Secretary, now Sir Bernard.

We were both at one of those enjoyable conferences
at Königswinter on the Rhine.
It was only a few weeks after Ted had lost the Tory leadership.
Our conference theme one afternoon
was "Democracy and the Media", or some such woolly subject.
Ted's intervention was avidly awaited.
Curtly and characteristically
he cut through the waffle.

"I wish to explain," he said,
"why political leaders lose elections
and get kicked out.
The reason is simple.
The people get bored by seeing the same politicians
interviewed so often on television
by the same boring interviewers."

Ted proceeded to propose a solution.
"Instead of getting rid of the boring politicians,
I have never understood why we cannot get rid
of the boring television interviewers."

For this somewhat extreme proposal,
I regret to report there was loud and prolonged applause.

Ted's sense of humour, which has always been faintly macabre,
is one of his most attractive qualities.
You never know whether he is being funny or not.

I have another endearing memory of Ted Heath.
Nearly 25 years ago at a general election
we had programmes called *Election Forum* on TV
in which the three party leaders each appeared
to answer questions chosen from thousands of postcards
sent in by the voters.

Suddenly, sorting through a bundle of cards
I came upon one
which I instantly realised was electoral dynamite.
In youthful handwriting,
addressed to the Rt Hon Edward Heath,

Leader of the Conservative Party, % the BBC, London W12,
the question on the card read as follows:

Dear Daddy,
When you get to No. 10, will you do
the decent thing
and invite Mummy and me to tea?

I held in my hand the key to a general election.
What on earth were we do to? After all, we were on the BBC,
which is always impartial.
Would it be impartial to use this question?
Would it be impartial *not* to use it?

We remembered Disraeli's comment
when he heard of an escapade of the ageing Lord Palmerston:
"If this gets out, he'll sweep the country."

I discussed our terrible dilemma
with my co-questioner, Ian Trethowan.
He displayed all the wisdom and prudence
which was later to make *him* Director-General of the BBC.

"Oh, we *must* use it," he said.
"But only in rehearsal." Which we did.

Mr Heath's response can now be revealed:
his shoulders shook with mirth, silent and non-committal.

But this is no time for frivolity.
We cannot ignore the political storm-clouds
overhanging this happy occasion.
No less a person than the redoubtable Sir John Stokes
has warned the 1922 Committee of a sinister development:
"Suddenly, people are beginning to talk politics in the pubs."

And if one believes *The Times* newspaper,
"Tory MPs are now in a state of subdued panic."
If so, some of them, including Mr Heath
(who is a former Chief Whip),
are old enough to remember the immortal words

of Rear-Admiral Sir Morgan Morgan-Giles:
"*Pro bono publico*, no bloody panico."

One of Ted Heath's favourite quotations
when he was Prime Minister
was Disraeli's famous remark about England:

> It is a very difficult country to move –
> a very difficult country indeed,
> and one in which there is more disappointment
> to be looked for than success.

That was said in 1881. A good many people in this room
may have come to the same conclusion in 1990.

But Ted Heath can surely feel immense pride, not disappointment,
in his 40 years as a Member of Parliament.
No one will deny him his supreme achievement
as the Prime Minister who took this country
into the European Community.
Thus did he fulfil his pledge of 1970
"to change the course of history in this country, nothing less".

This great gathering of friends and fellow-statesmen,
of colleagues, contemporaries, and critics,
is a fitting tribute to his courage, his tenacity and his vision.

But this is not a memorial service.
Ted Heath is in magnificent health, and fighting fit.
He will continue to say what he thinks,
without fear or favour, for many years to come,
from that place of his below the gangway,
so near to, and yet so far from,
the seat of power on the Treasury bench.

So please pencil in your diaries another luncheon
for Mr Heath like this in February 2000.
Meanwhile, on your 40th parliamentary birthday, Ted,
congratulations, and many happy returns.

arch 7th, 1990 at the Middle Temple. This was the occasion on which I was made an "Honorary Bencher" of the Middle Temple. The "Benchers" of each Inn of Court are the judges and senior barristers who run its affairs.

I had practised as a barrister for only 18 months. It was therefore an immense honour when the Benchers of the Middle Temple elected me to join them as an Honorary Bencher in 1990.

There was a dinner in the magnificent Middle Temple Hall, in which Shakespeare's *Twelfth Night* is reputed to have had its first performance in 1601, and in which I was called to the Bar in 1952. In the ceremony of "Call to the Bench" after dinner, the newly called Bencher has, by custom, to "give an account of himself" in a short speech to his fellow Benchers.

On this evening, my audience numbered about 50 Benchers – Law Lords, High Court judges, Queen's Counsel, retired judges – all learned in the law, and expert in advocacy. A daunting audience.

Happily, several old friends and contemporaries of mine were present. The Bencher who gracefully presided was the distinguished Chancery barrister Leo Price, QC, whom I had known since our undergraduate time at Oxford.

Benchers are properly called "Masters of the Bench". They are addressed in the Inn as "Master". Hence the references in my speech to Master (Sir Geoffrey) Howe, Master (Sir Patrick) Mayhew (the Attorney General), Master (Lord) Donaldson, Master (Sir Ronald) Waterhouse, etc. And now there was Master Day!

Master Treasurer:

Before such a gathering as this,
so learned in the law,
and so practised in eloquence,
you will understand that in giving this account of myself,
I speak with even more than my usual humility.

To have been called to the Bench
under *your* auspices, Master Treasurer,
is an honour which gives me particular pleasure.
I have known and admired you for over 40 years,
ever since we were undergraduates together
in Oxford's golden post-war age.

I was always greatly impressed by the precision
of your brain, and of your diction.
I know you to be a man of unswerving principle and purpose.

On one occasion, alas, in your distant youth,
your frank and forthright manner was your undoing.
You were being interviewed, perhaps in this very room,
as an applicant for a Harmsworth Scholarship.
One of the venerable Benchers said,
"Mr Price, I see that at Oxford
you were President of the Conservative Association?"
"Yes, sir."
"And you were elected Treasurer of the Oxford Union?"
"Yes, sir."
"Mr Price, which would you rather be:
Prime Minister or Lord Chancellor?"

Your answer, Master Treasurer,
came without prevarication or hesitation.
And the Harmsworth went to somebody else.

The Bench to which I have been called
includes some very old friends, such as Master Howe,
Master Waterhouse, Master Mayhew, Master Mildon
and Master Richardson.

Master Waterhouse, Master Howe and I
were called to the "utter" Bar in this Hall
by Earl Jowitt
(with stately wing-collars up to his ears)
on the same evening: February 5th, 1952.

Unlike me, Master Howe and Master Waterhouse
were destined for the glittering prizes,

whereas I was to sink
into the obscurity of the television studios.
It is Master Waterhouse whom you must blame
for my career in television.
One summer lunchtime in 1955
he saw pinned up on an Inn notice-board the following:
"ITN" – of which I had never heard –
"are looking for newscasters." A word I did not understand.
"The post may be of interest
to members of the Bar
thinking of giving up practice"
which by then I had already done.

I applied. I was auditioned. I was appointed –
much to my surprise.
So I suddenly found that I was not only in a new career,
but was helping to create a new and unknown force in society –
the electronic journalism of television.

My experience as a barrister in Court was minimal,
but it left a lasting impression on me.
The strain of appearing on television
to interview Prime Ministers before millions
has been nothing compared to what I suffered
when trying to say something at the Central Criminal Court
in mitigation of sentence on a man with several previous convictions
for robbery with violence – especially when the judge
was the late Mr Justice Hilbery.

But contrary to what the press have often suggested,
the Old Bailey and Lime Grove
have never had anything in common.
The professional interrogation of the courtroom
has never been transplantable to the television studio.

The most obvious difference is *time*.
The longest television interview
is less than an hour, usually only a few minutes.
Whereas counsel in court can cross-examine at length.

The television interviewer is subject

to no professional code of conduct.
And in a television studio
there is no judge to ensure fair play.

But, most importantly, in a television interview
the witness is never on oath.
It would be bad taste to speculate
whether some answers on television might have been different
if the politicians concerned had been on oath.

But despite these obvious differences
between courtroom and studio,
I have been offered much advice by barristers and judges.

The press and politicians have often complained
about "trial by TV" and "ruthless inquisitions".
Yet barristers and judges have often condemned
my questions as soft, superficial and wet.

Some years ago, I was buttonholed
by a veteran practitioner of the cross-examiner's art:

"Well, you let that shyster off the hook last night."
(The said "shyster" was a senior Cabinet Minister.)
"Oh dear," I said. "I thought I'd pressed him
rather vigorously. What should I have done?"

"You should have said:
'Secretary of State, did you *hear* my question?
You did? I'm much obliged.
Did you understand my question? You did?
Now will you be kind enough to answer my question?'"

I am keeping that particular technique in reserve –
for my last interview.

I remember a senior High Court judge
giving me advice on how to begin an interview
that evening with the then Prime Minister.
The *policy* areas, I said, were fairly obvious
but my problem was how to *begin*.
(I should mention that the Prime Minister concerned

was not – how shall I put it? –
at the height of his reputation.)
The old judge, veteran of many a *cause célèbre,*
reflected for a moment and said:
"You should begin by asking him this.
'Does the word *shame* mean anything to you?'"
I must confess that after due consideration
I chickened out.

Though I gave up the Bar, Master Treasurer,
I did not sever all connection with the law,
nor with this ancient Inn.
For several years in the 1970s
I served, along with Master Hodgson,
on the Committee on the Law of Contempt of Court,
chaired by the late Master Phillimore.
A most enjoyable and absorbing task.
We conducted our deliberations
in the room adjoining this Parliament chamber,
and took our lunch in this hall.

On that Contempt Committee, I had the pleasure
of interrogating Master Donaldson.
This was during that remarkable period of his career
when he was President of the ill-fated
National Industrial Relations Court.
There were, I remember, some interesting questions
for Master Donaldson about the "Pentonville Five",
and the official Solicitor,
who had suddenly popped up from nowhere.

I also had on that Committee the great honour
to question Master Denning,
Master of the Rolls, as he then was.
I forget the exact point, but I said, "But Lord Denning,
that section of the Administration of Justice Act
quite clearly says something else, does it not?"
Lord Denning replied, "Oh, does it really?
Well, we'll 'ave to get round that some'ow, won't we?"

Master Treasurer, in your initial letter to me

you pointed out that "the Bar and Inns of Court
have enjoyed a poor public image"
during the controversy over
the Government's Green and White Papers
and the Lord Chancellor's bill
to reform the legal profession.
Certainly the great profession here represented
no longer seems to be regarded
with the same respect and reverence as in the past.
And I regret to say that in the heated debate
of this last year the leaders of this profession
have not always won high marks for advocacy.

Now I happen to share the view of those
who argue that Lord Mackay's so-called reforms
may in the long term endanger
the standards of justice, because in the end
the standards of justice must depend on the quality
and character of the Bar,
on whom the judges rely for argument,
and from which the judges of the future are drawn.

That seems to me the essential point.
But public and parliamentary opinion
does not yet appear to have been convinced
that such a danger may exist.

Many of our legislators do not seem much concerned
to uphold what Thomas Erskine famously called
"the dignity, independence and integrity
of the English Bar, without which impartial justice,
the most valuable part of our constitution,
can have no existence".

I am sure Master Mayhew will bear that in mind
when the Bill comes before the Commons' House.

Master Treasurer, the honour you have done me
is one especially valued by me
because I am not the kind of person
who is normally made an Honorary Bencher.

I am not of the Royal House.
I have not been a Prime Minister,
nor am I a statesman of any kind.
I am not an ambassador, nor a mandarin,
nor an academic, nor a bishop.
Nor have I achieved eminence
in any of the other learned professions.

I am merely a failed member
of your own profession and of your own Inn.
I do not know if I am the first failed barrister
to have been made an Honorary Bencher,
but I am deeply conscious
of the signal honour you have done me tonight.

23 THE MIRACLE OF MAY 10TH, 1940

May 11th, 1990. The Churchill Club of Manchester, which was founded to honour the memory of Sir Winston Churchill, held this dinner to commemorate the 50th anniversary of the formation of his wartime coalition government in 1940. I had been invited to speak by his grandson, my friend and neighbour, Winston Churchill, then MP for Davyhulme. Rather than deliver another panegyric about his grandfather, I decided to tell the dramatic story, hour by hour, of May 10th, 1940, the day that Churchill became Prime Minister.

Many in my audience – staunch Lancashire Conservatives – were probably surprised to be told that if the Tory establishment had had its way, Churchill would never have become Prime Minister in 1940.

I refer in this lecture to the unforgettable impact of Churchill's war broadcasts. Later, I was fascinated to learn of the peculiar form of speech script which he used throughout his political life. This was known to Churchill's staff as "speech form" or "psalm form". Here are two opening sentences of his broadcast on May 19th, 1940, exactly as they were typed for him to deliver:

> I speak to you for the first time as Prime Minister
> in a solemn hour
> for the life of our country,
> of our Empire,
> of our Allies and – above all –
>
> of the cause of freedom.
>
> A tremendous battle is raging in France and Flanders.[1]

---

[1] That historic script is fully reproduced in *The Churchill War Papers*, Volume 2, by Sir Martin Gilbert, whom I thank for permission to use this quotation.

This Churchillian form has since been adopted by many lesser speech-makers, including myself for as long as I can remember. That is why my speeches in this book are printed not as normal prose but looking like blank verse. This follows the form in which my speeches have invariably been typed for me. The varying length of lines and the odd arrangement of words are to suit the rhythm and emphasis of the speaker, and to catch his eye easily. Not truly psalm-like, perhaps, but helpful for me, not least for this Churchill lecture.

Members of the Churchill Club of Manchester:

My only qualification for speaking to you tonight
is one which I share with many of you,
that I have youthful memories, ineradicable memories,
of Winston Churchill as our wartime Prime Minister
when to me he was the greatest of Englishmen.

I am proud to be able to tell my teenage sons
that I was taken by my father to hear him speak
before the war when I was a boy of ten,
when he was out of office and in the wilderness.

I am proud to tell my sons also
that I met him once, briefly, when he was PM
and in his 80th year.

Not, of course, for a TV interview.
No one ever did that. He had no truck with television.

What we are marking tonight is no ordinary anniversary.

What occurred on Friday, May 10th, 1940
was a climacteric of British history –
one of the fateful moments
when the destiny of the British people
was in the lap of the gods.

It is a thrilling story: the story of how
Winston Leonard Spencer Churchill
became the King's First Minister that day.

It may now seem inevitable that Churchill
should have become PM in 1940.
It certainly seemed so to me
as an all-knowing schoolboy
who was 16 years old at the time.

Was he not the obvious man for the job?
Overwhelmingly qualified by his experience of war,
by his stand against appeasement,
by his pre-war warnings of Hitler's intentions,
by his stature as a parliamentarian,
by his mastery of the English language?
Obvious? Inevitable? No: what happened on May 10th, 1940
was a *miracle*, considering the distrust and suspicion
which Churchill then aroused in the political establishment,
in the Tory Party itself, in the Labour Party,
at Buckingham Palace, in Whitehall.

To quote Sir John Colville, his private secretary:

> Seldom can a PM have taken office
> with the Establishment … so dubious of the choice
> and so prepared to find its doubts justified.

The Establishment's house-organ, *The Times*,
had long been pro-appeasement and anti-Churchill.
And he was seldom allowed to broadcast on the pre-war BBC.

There was contemptuous hostility towards him
among prominent Conservatives.
On the evening of May 10th, 1940,
the very evening when the King had sent for Churchill,
Colville's diary records a private conversation with R A Butler,
then the Foreign Office Minister in the Commons.

Rab denounced Churchill as
"… the greatest adventurer in modern political history"

and as "a half-breed American".

Rab said:
"... this sudden coup of Winston and his rabble
was a serious and unnecessary disaster."

Why was there so much Tory distrust of Churchill?
He had acquired a reputation for being erratic
and impetuous and brilliant.
The British do not much care for brilliance in a politician.
They tend to prefer a "safe pair of hands"!

And Churchill had clashed time and again
with pre-war Tory governments –
over India, over the abdication of Edward VIII,
and over the Munich Agreement –
which had made many doubt his judgement.

Indeed, had he died or retired before 1939,
historians would have written him off as a brilliant failure.

So strong in 1940 was the Tory distrust of Churchill
that it even persisted for several weeks
after he had become PM – right up till early July.

Churchill writes:

> Till that moment, the Conservative Party
> in the Commons treated me with some reserve
> ... it was from the Labour Party that I received
> the warmest welcome when I entered the House.

At the beginning of May, the disastrous campaign in Norway
had made it doubtful that Chamberlain could survive.
The preference then of leading Tories, almost without exception,
was for Lord Halifax, the Foreign Secretary,
former Viceroy of India, chief accomplice
in appeasement, and man of Munich.

There was also much support for Halifax among the *Labour Party* leaders.
They still could not forgive Churchill for his tough line

during the General Strike, nor for having sent troops
to the South Wales mining area of Tonypandy in 1910.

The biographer of Clement Attlee claims
that Attlee himself was for Churchill.
But when Chamberlain was about to resign,
Attlee and the Labour leaders did not specify Churchill
rather than Halifax to be Prime Minister of a coalition.

Labour's prime objective was to get Chamberlain out.
Chamberlain seemed more likely to make way
for Halifax than for Churchill.

There's no doubt whom the Palace wanted.
When Chamberlain resigned on May 10th,
the very day Hitler had invaded Holland and Belgium,
the King recorded in his diary:

> We had an informal talk about his successor
> and I of course suggested Halifax
> but he told me H was not enthusiastic,
> as being in the Lords he could only act as a shadow
> or a ghost in the Commons where all the real
> work took place. I was disappointed by this statement
> as I thought Halifax was the obvious man and that his
> peerage could be placed in abeyance for the time being ..."

All this anti-Churchill feeling was characteristically summed up
by Churchill's closest personal friend in politics, Lord Beaverbrook:

> Chamberlain wanted Halifax, Labour wanted Halifax,
> Sinclair wanted Halifax. The Lords wanted Halifax.
> The King wanted Halifax. And Halifax wanted Halifax.

But in that last jibe there was more malice than justice.
For (as you'll hear in a moment)
when it came to the crunch,
Halifax firmly and wisely ruled himself out.

How long Halifax would have survived or, more to the point,
how long *Britain* would have survived under Halifax,
is another question.

But how was it that Neville Chamberlain was made to go?

Here I must remind you that
the resignation of Chamberlain is the only occasion
when a British Prime Minister in good health,
and commanding a majority in the House of Commons,
has been forced out of office.
I am not saying it could never happen again.[1]
I am not saying it could.
I am making no prediction of any kind.
I cannot foresee the future.

But what was it that brought Chamberlain down?
Not backstairs intrigue or conspiratorial plotting.
It was an open and spontaneous revolt
of Tory back-benchers in the division lobbies
of the House of Commons.

The revolt came on Wednesday, May 8th,
at the end of the momentous two-day debate
on the ill-fated Norway campaign.

The vote was to sweep Chamberlain from power.
The government's majority, normally over 200,
was slashed to 81.

Though he won the vote that night,
Chamberlain suffered a fatal haemorrhage of support.
Some 41 of his supporters voted against him.
About 60 other Tory MPs abstained.

Among the Tory MPs who courageously defied
their party's three-line whip and voted against Chamberlain
were Leo Amery, Duff Cooper, Lady Astor,

---

[1] I must have had a prescient feeling! Because it did happen again, only six months after I gave this
lecture, in November 1990, when Margaret Thatcher was forced out of office.

Admiral of the Fleet Sir Roger Keyes, Quintin Hogg,
Robert Boothby, Harold Macmillan, and a 24–year–old Army officer
who had only just been elected, John Profumo.

When the result of the vote was announced,
there were noisy scenes of exultation in the Chamber,
which Rab Butler called "distasteful".
Harold Macmillan joined in singing *Rule Britannia*.

Next day, Thursday, May 9th, Chamberlain summoned Attlee
and Greenwood to No. 10 and asked them
if they would serve under him as Prime Minister of a Coalition.
Churchill and Halifax were there too.

Attlee describes it as "incredible"
that Chamberlain still seemed to think he could hang on.
Attlee spoke bluntly to him:
"The Labour Party won't have you and
I think the country won't have you."

To this, Chamberlain did not, at first, reply.
Chamberlain then asked if Labour
would serve under *another* Conservative PM.
Attlee said he thought so, but he wished first to consult his colleagues,
who were then at their party conference in Bournemouth.
Attlee and Greenwood left to go to Bournemouth.

Churchill and Halifax remained with Chamberlain.
And Churchill describes the historic conversation thus:

> I have had many important interviews in
> my public life, and this was certainly
> the most important. Usually I talk a
> great deal but on this occasion I was silent.

According to Lord Halifax's note of the conversation,
Chamberlain suggested that Halifax was more acceptable
to the Labour Party than Churchill.
And Chamberlain looked at Churchill and asked:
"Can you see any reason, Winston, why
in these days a peer should not be PM?"

This, as Churchill at once saw, was a trap question.
If he said, "*Yes,* I can see several reasons why not,"
that would be openly demanding the premiership for himself.
If he said, "*No*" (PM in Lords no problem)
he knew Chamberlain could at once say,
"Since Winston agrees I'll advise the King
to send for Edward [Lord Halifax]."

So Churchill said nothing. He turned his back
and gazed out over Horse Guards Parade.

There was a very long silent pause,
which seemed longer (says Churchill)
that the two minutes' silence on Armistice Day.

According to Churchill's account:

> Halifax said that he felt that his
> position as a Peer, out of the House
> of Commons, would make it very
> difficult for him to discharge the
> duties of PM in a war like this ...
> and by the time he had finished it was
> clear that the duty would fall upon me.

That night – or in the early hours of next morning, Friday, May 10th –
Hitler invaded Holland and Belgium. The blitzkrieg had begun.

In 10 Downing Street, the War Cabinet met at 8am.
There were to be three Cabinet meetings that day.

Meanwhile in the Highcliff Hotel in Bournemouth,
Labour's NEC agreed their answers to the two questions
which Attlee had undertaken to ask his colleagues.

First: are you prepared to join a Government led by Chamberlain?
The answer was *No.*

Second: would you be prepared to serve under somebody else?
The answer was *Yes.*

Attlee read these answers over the phone
to No. 10 from Bournemouth at about 5pm
and then caught the 5.15 train back to Waterloo.

In Downing Street at that moment,
the War Cabinet was in session for the third time that day.
Attlee's message was given to Chamberlain in the Cabinet Room.

The PM finished the agenda. Then he read
to his colleagues Attlee's answer:
"In the light of that answer, I have decided
to tender my resignation at once."

Thus it was *Labour's* answer which finally forced Chamberlain to resign.
But you'll notice that Labour did not insist on Churchill.

Half an hour later, at the Palace, Chamberlain advised the King
"to send for Winston and ask him to form a Government".

When Churchill arrived, the two men, the monarch and the statesman,
first indulged in a little frivolous banter
of the kind which famous men enjoy at moments of crisis.
According to Churchill's account:

> His Majesty … looked at me searchingly and quizzically for some
>   moments,
> and then said, "I suppose you don't know why I have sent for
>   you?"
> Adopting his mood, I replied, "Sir, I simply couldn't imagine
>   why."
> The King laughed and said,
> "I want to ask you to form a Government."
> I said I would certainly do so.

Churchill told the King that he would immediately send
for the leaders of the Labour and Liberal Parties,
that he'd form a War Cabinet of five or six members,
and that he hoped to have the names by midnight.

Meanwhile, Attlee arrived at Waterloo station
from Bournemouth at 9pm.

He was met by a Downing Street emissary
who told him the new Prime Minister
was anxious to see him as soon as possible.

And so at a meeting which lasted far into the night,
they began to form the great all-party wartime coalition.

At the age of 65, when most men have been put out to grass,
Winston Churchill came into his own.
He seized control of the supreme direction of the war.
He was not only Prime Minister but also Minister of Defence
and Leader of the House of Commons.

The kaleidoscopic character of his political career
had uniquely fitted him to lead an all-party Government.

Originally (in the reign of Queen Victoria)
he was *Tory* MP for Oldham. Then a *Liberal*. Later a *Constitutionalist*.
Then a *Conservative* again.
Churchill had always been at heart something of an independent.

Sir Winston said on one occasion,
"During my life I have often had to eat my own words,
and I have always found them a wholesome diet."

And he could justly claim in his war memoirs
that when he came to form the coalition government,
"Eleven years in the political wilderness
had freed me from ordinary party antagonisms."

That night, May 10th, 1940, it was not until 3am
that the new Prime Minister got to bed.

At that moment, as he later recalled,

> I was conscious of a profound sense of relief.
> At last I had the authority
> to give directions over the whole scene.
> I felt as if I was walking with destiny
> and that all my past life
> had been but a preparation

for this hour and for this trial.

At once he galvanised the machinery of Government
and stirred the spirit of the British people.
He "mobilised the English language and sent it into battle".[1]

Those wireless broadcasts of his
will never be forgotten by those who heard them.
I heard every one, either at school or in the Army.
That voice – I can hear it now –
that rasping, lisping, growling, declamatory voice.
Those words which gave us faith in ultimate victory –
words which will live as long as the English language.
Those rolling sentences with their marvellous mixture
of plain, basic, down-to-earth English and baroque oratory
in the style inspired by Gibbon and Macaulay.

If Winston Churchill had *not* become Prime Minister
on that day 50 years ago,
the probable consequences for this nation
are dreadful to contemplate:
perhaps a "negotiated peace", with a surrender
on humiliating terms by some British Pétain;
the occupation of these islands,
repression and tyranny of the foulest type,
aided and abetted no doubt by some British fifth-column
of Nazi sympathisers, and by appeasers in high places.

Do not forget that in the dark days of May 1940
the possibility of a peace settlement with Hitler
had to be considered by the War Cabinet.
Opinions were divided. Churchill was emphatically against.
He warned that *any* peace settlement
would put us completely at Hitler's mercy.
He told Halifax that the chances of getting terms
which would not enslave us were 1,000 to one against.

Of course Churchill *considered* a negotiated peace,

[1] A quotation from Edward R. Murrow, the great American broadcaster, which was later used by President Kennedy.

so desperate was Britain's situation,
and so delicate was his own position as Prime Minister.
But he considered it only to reject it.

His unwavering opposition was fortified
by an astonishing demonstration of support
from a meeting of 25 ministers not in the War Cabinet.

Labour's Hugh Dalton was present. In his diary, Dalton says Churchill
was "quite magnificent", telling them:

> "... that if we had to make peace now
> we would become a slave state
> with a puppet British Government
> under Mosley or some such person.
> Every one of you would rise up
> and tear me down from my place
> if I were for one moment
> to contemplate parley or surrender.
>
> If this long island story of ours
> is to end at last,
> let it end only when each of us
> lies choking in his own blood upon the ground."

Churchill writes that the ministers jumped up
and ran to him, shouting their approval and patting him on the back.

It was one of the most extraordinary scenes of the war,
at one of the darkest moments of the war.

I was fortunate, when a young man in the BBC,
to hear Sir Winston speak on his 80th birthday
in 1954 in Westminister Hall.
That was when he was honoured by the whole House of Commons
for his long parliamentary service
and for leading the nation to victory in war.

But Sir Winston modestly protested:
"... it was a nation and race dwelling all around the globe
that had the lion's heart. I had the luck to be called upon

to give the roar."

He was presented on that occasion
with a somewhat controversial portrait,[1]
but also with a birthday book signed by virtually every MP.
Inside that book were inscribed some words
from *The Pilgrim's Progress* by John Bunyan:

> You have been so faithful and so loving to us,
> you have fought so stoutly for us,
> you have been so hearty in counselling of us,
> that we shall never forget your favour towards us.

Ladies and Gentlemen of the Churchill Club: thank you.

---

[1] The brilliant but unflattering portrait by Graham Sutherland, cruelly depicting WSC in his old age, not in his prime. It was destroyed by Clementine Churchill – understandably, but sadly depriving us of a historic work of art.

ROBERT CARVEL, 1919–1990

F riday, 8th July, 1990, St John's United Reform Church, Northwood.

A thanksgiving service for the life of Robert Carvel. He was the long-time political correspondent of the *Evening Standard*, and a regular broadcaster on BBC radio.

He was also one of the best-loved characters on the Westminster scene. When, at the age of 71, he died from a heart attack, I lost a great personal and professional friend.

The thanksgiving service was held immediately after his private funeral. This made it an even more poignant occasion than a thanksgiving service usually is. I was acutely aware that his newly bereaved widow, Florence, was present, as also were his son, John Carvel, the *Guardian* journalist, and his two grandsons. But I knew that Bob Carvel would not have wanted me to give a humourless or depressing address.

When I was told that Bob Carvel had died,
that shocked and saddened me more
than any news I had heard for many a year.

My two teenage sons were with me
when I got the phone call.
They had never met him or heard of him.
But they could see I was dreadfully upset.
I tried to explain how we had worked together
and what he was.

I tried to tell them
he was a great political journalist, a brilliant broadcaster.
That would not have meant very much to them.
So I told them simply that Bob Carvel
had been a good friend to me for over 30 years,

not just a hullo-nice-to-see-you-again friend,
but a real friend, a kind friend, a generous friend,
a wise friend, an honest friend and a *funny* friend.

Though this is a very sad occasion,
I have a feeling, knowing Bob as I did,
that he would not have wanted it
to be *too* solemn or too mournful.
I don't think he would have wanted us
to leave this church depressed or miserable.
He would have been pleased to think
that at this thanksgiving service
we would remember happily
his merry wit, his mischievous humour,
the warmth and sparkle of his company.

Many of you here are much better fitted than I
to speak about Bob Carvel,
about his qualities as a journalist,
about his talents as a broadcaster.
In the BBC he was held in high affection and esteem.

I have never been a newspaper man –
except briefly (as Bob would remind me)
when I wrote a column for the old *News Chronicle*.
He would say, usually late at night
when (as I thought) he was losing an argument,
"What do *you* know about it? The only newspaper
you ever wrote for closed down as a result!"
To which I never had a convincing retort.

My long friendship with Bob was forged
by more than heated arguments, and gossip
about politics and personalities.
I talked to him in the press gallery tea-room,
or on the telephone, at almost every critical moment of my life,
either to get advice,
or to be cheered up,
or to report good news. He was the first person I told
that I was going to be married.
He was the first person to whom

I proudly announced that I was to be a father.

And it was Bob Carvel whom I first told in 1959
that I had become a Liberal Candidate.
That, incidentally, was the only occasion
I can remember him being flattering rather than frank.
Instead of saying what he should have said
(that I was a reckless ass) he said,
"Robin, you're a very courageous fellow."

He loved our frequent discussions
to do with contractual negotiations
with the BBC, especially about fees.
I remember one contract we discussed
walking along the promenade at Blackpool in 1978.
It concerned *The World at One*,
of which I eventually became the presenter
only because Bob Carvel decided to turn the offer down.
A fact of which he never hesitated to remind me!

Bob Carvel resisted more than one tempting offer
from the BBC to be a full-time radio commentator.
But he remained devoted to his newspaper, the *Evening Standard*.
He was a master of his craft,
the elder statesman of the lobby correspondents.

His old master and mentor, Lord Beaverbrook,
was fond of quoting from Rudyard Kipling's poem on the press,
which has a verse which goes:

> He has lit his pipe in the morning calm
> That follows the midnight stress –
> He hath sold his heart to the old Black Art
> We call the daily Press.

Bob, of course, was an *evening* newspaperman
who would light *his* pipe in the *afternoon* calm
after the mid*day* stress.
But nonetheless (you may think) Kipling had Carvel in mind.

Though he remained faithful to the *Evening Standard*,

he loved the oral journalism
of what he persisted in calling "the wireless".
His broadcasting style was unique,
combining authority with irreverence.

His generosity to colleagues was legendary.
Many a fledgling BBC producer was guided gently
by Bob Carvel into the ways of Westminster.
And he would even give up time to be my sparring partner.
Before some big TV interview of mine,
he would play with relish the part
of Harold Wilson, or Ted Heath or Margaret Thatcher.
These verbal fencing matches, in the press gallery tea-room,
would start off seriously and realistically.
Then the questions would get tougher,
Bob's answers would get rougher,
and gradually a small audience of colleagues
would gather around the table
as the mock interview became more heated and abusive,
with Robert ordering me not to be impertinent,
or to sharpen my wits.

In such ways was Bob Carvel generous
with his experience, with his time, with his judgement.

One reason for his greatness as a political journalist
was that he loved his work, he loved Parliament, he loved politics.
I don't think he loved all politicians.
But he was certainly not one of those journalists
who despise politicians as a breed.
He knew that Parliament was a workshop
as well as a theatre, whose proceedings were not
staged solely for the benefit of the press gallery.

Many parliamentarians are as proud as I am
to have been his friend. Bob knew many famous front-benchers
from the day that they first entered the House.
He watched them win and he watched them lose.
And he reported on their progress
from maiden speakers and nervous back-benchers
to Privy Counsellors and Cabinet Ministers,

like a shrewd old schoolmaster looking at generation
after generation of pupils.
And he gave them much good political advice and instruction.

For over 40 years, Bob Carvel himself
was part of the political process of this country,
depicting the dramas, interpreting the crises, predicting the storms.

A typical Bob Carvel exclusive
on the *Evening Standard* front page, written at 6am,
would tell us at noon what the Cabinet
(which would be in "deep disarray") was now deciding.
MPs assembling at Westminster
would read with fascination that they were "in angry mood",
"baying for" this or that "Minister's blood".

He was a vivid writer of news,
and also a numerate analyst of politics.
In the modern science of psephology,
he was a match for David Butler and Robert McKenzie.

He revelled in by-elections and party conferences.
Many a boring election, many a tedious press conference,
has been brought to life or reduced to farce
by Bob's irreverent and exquisitely timed intervention.
He might suddenly ask, for example,
"Would the Chairman of the Party
tell us why he's looking so miserable?"

One of the most memorable Carvellisms
was at the Warrington by-election of 1981.
Harold Wilson had come to speak for the Labour Candidate
against Roy Jenkins of the SDP.[1]
At the news conference someone asked,
"But Mr Wilson, wasn't Roy Jenkins a good Chancellor
in your great Labour Government?"
Wilson replied, "Yes, he was very good. But he kept office hours."
At which Bob Carvel snapped his notebook shut

---

[1] The Social Democratic Party, founded earlier in 1981 by Jenkins, Shirley Williams, David Owen and Bill Rodgers, was approaching the crest of its brief wave.

and whispered loudly, "That's the story, boys:
Wilson too weak to sack lazy Chancellor."

He was an accomplished extractor of secrets from politicians.
He was also a great *keeper* of secrets,
of the secrets entrusted to him.
For many a public figure would confide in Bob.
But he kept, closely guarded, secrets of his *own* life.
I never succeeded in discovering from him
what exactly he did in the war.
I cross-examined him about it many times,
but he revelled in being mysterious
about his shadowy, cloak-and-dagger,
hush-hush exploits
in Army intelligence in occupied France and in Northern Ireland.

His reticence, he realised only too well,
was tantalising in the extreme
and whetted one's appetite for more.
But something he could not keep secret,
though he modestly kept very quiet about it.
It was not mentioned in his newspaper obituaries.
This was the decoration he had been awarded
for meritorious Army service in Northern Ireland.

Bob Carvel liked to call himself a republican.
He cared not a fig for honours or gongs,
although he recommended a number of colleagues for honours
which he would himself have refused.
But in the King's Birthday Honours for 1946,
the British Empire Medal was awarded
(on the recommendation of the Northern Ireland Command)
to Robert Burns Carvel, Sgt RA.

Robert *Burns* Carvel – and that was another family secret
he never advertised, that he was named after another Scottish writer.

And being a canny Scot, he would guard
his *professional* secrets carefully.
In those far-off days in the '60s,
the days of the great London evening-paper battles,

his leading rival was John Dickinson of the *Evening News*.
Dickinson was asked what sort of relationship
he had with Bob Carvel. "Oh," he said,
"We have a splendid relationship.
I tell Bob everything I know. He tells me nothing."

His reporting of politics in the *Evening Standard*
or on the BBC was always scrupulously fair
but at the same time (and this was his gift) incisive and pungent.

The story goes (some of you may have read it
in the *Evening Standard* the other day)
that his sense of fairness dates from his youth in Glasgow.
It is said that he would write impassioned letters
to the local paper every second week
attacking the evils of playing golf on the Sabbath.
Every other week (under another name)
he would write equally fervent letters
defending the healthy virtues of a Sunday round of golf.
This correspondence rolled on for months,
and displayed three of the qualities
which endeared Bob to us all throughout the rest of his life:
a gift with words, the ability to see both sides of an argument,
and a lovable sense of mischief.

At this service of thanksgiving, our hearts go out
to Florence, his beloved wife.
And to his son, John, and to his grandsons.
We share their grief.
We shall miss him very much.

Whenever I think of my old sparring partner,
which I will fondly and frequently,
the memory of him will make me smile.
What better legacy could a man
leave to his friends?

25 A SCHOOL PRIZE-GIVING

December 1st, 1990 at Arnold House School in London, where my elder son, Alexander, was a pupil. It was the annual speech day, or prize-giving.

I have presented prizes at several schools in my time. The ceremonies can be somewhat tedious. And the presenter of prizes usually makes a speech which sends most of his audience, particularly the boys or girls or both, to sleep.

I was determined not to send anyone to sleep. Fortunately, events came to my rescue. As luck would have it, they – the events – gave me wonderful opportunities for topical remarks. This prize-giving took place only three days after John Major had succeeded Margaret Thatcher on November 28th as Prime Minister.

For the previous two or three weeks the Tory leadership contest had been the big talking point and was the topical background to my speech as presenter of school prizes on December 1st. The result of the second ballot was John Major 185, Michael Heseltine 131, Douglas Hurd 56, whereupon Heseltine conceded and withdrew. John Major went to the Palace next morning and was now Prime Minister.

All this, thanks to saturation TV and press coverage, was fresh in the minds of my audience, even in the minds of some of the young boys. This was a godsend to the speech-maker and prize-presenter, who milked it for all he was worth.

Here we had a political sensation which, as I explain, was unprecedented. This would be a perfect preamble to the personal reminiscence and educational thoughts expected of me.

Parents, teachers and boys enjoyed it uproariously, with the boys, taking their cue from the grown-ups, laughing more and more as it went along.

Headmaster, Ladies and Gentlemen, and Boys:

I prefer not to begin by creating trouble.
That is not in my nature. But I am puzzled
as to what is expected of me on this occasion.

What sort of speech am I to make?
Is it to be congratulatory?
Is it to be entertaining –
a comic turn?
Is it to be reminiscent –
stories of misspent youth?
Is it to be an uplifting sermon?

If my duty is to be congratulatory,
that duty is also my pleasure.
I sincerely congratulate all those boys who won prizes,
and with equal sincerity I congratulate those,
if any, who did not,
for so manfully concealing their disappointment.

The trouble with prizes is that not everyone can win them.
If there are winners, there have to be losers.
If you doubt the truth of that profound observation,
ask Michael Heseltine or Douglas Hurd.

I congratulate all the parents present
on their gifted sons, and on their good judgement
in choosing to send them
to such an excellent school as Arnold House.

I congratulate the members of staff
on their collective and individual labours
in achieving the excellence
which has had its culmination this afternoon.
Especially the musical overture, conducted so brilliantly
by Mrs Teresa Burman, who is the only conductor
I have ever seen who conducts as if
she were administering corporal punishment.

And, of course, I congratulate the Headmaster

on his leadership and guidance,
which has been as firm and wise and far-sighted as ever,
or so he tells me.

Headmasters have indeed a heavy responsibility.
I noticed the other day
an interesting new development in education.
It was about the first Headmaster to accept "performance-related pay".
Mr John Atkins, Headmaster of a school in Bromley,
is to receive an extra £2,000 a year on his salary
"if he shows that he has met the targets set down
by his school governors regarding curriculum,
learning experience, staffing, appraisal, staff development,
pupil support, activities outside school and resource management".

I am sure that Mr Jonathan Clegg needs no such incentive.
Were he to move to a performance-related contract
under which he would be paid by results at Arnold House,
he would soon become a millionaire.

If my speech is expected to be in any way entertaining,
then you will be disappointed.
I, alas, have never been one of those broadcasters
who bring laughter into your hearts,
or happiness into your homes.
I have been a herald of conflict and gloom,
a messenger of misery. I am a very dull dog indeed.
An elderly reporter of politics, one who has watched
the dramatic events of recent days with mounting incredulity
(which means that I could hardly believe it was happening).

Make no mistake about it,
we have just witnessed a climacteric –
a crucial turning-point – in British history.
Not only the end of an epoch,
but an *extraordinary* end of an *extraordinary* epoch.

What happened to Mrs Thatcher last week had never happened before.
For the first time ever in peacetime,
a British Prime Minister in good health,
commanding a majority in the House of Commons,

has been kicked out of office.

And what an extraordinary epoch the Thatcher years have been:
whether you are sad or glad to see her go,
she is the only Prime Minister whose name has been given to an "ism".

No one ever talked of Churchillism,
Macmillanism, Heathism or even Disraeli-ism.
As Mrs Thatcher tearfully remarked
to her very last Cabinet meeting,
"It's a funny old world."

The gripping drama of the last three weeks
has led the newspapers to mix some funny old metaphors.
I think I have read, "The Galloping Major
is now astride his mount
at the top of the greasy pole."
And this one: "Tarzan has been hoist
with his own petard and gets the poisoned chalice."

Now politics is back to normal.
Won't it be dull? The blood-letting is over.
Unity is breaking out.
The Cabinet is once again a mutual admiration society –
not surprising, as it is now all-male.

But forgive me, Headmaster, for this digression,
and for having delayed the keenly awaited
reminiscent portion of my speech,
in which I will talk about my distant youth.

I will give you only a brief summary.
Those of you who want more details
are referred to my memoirs. The paperback edition
is now available in all good bookshops
at only £5.99.
It is the ideal Christmas present
for anyone you don't really like
but can't overlook.

As to my youth, I must be frank.

I must confess to you that during my school-days
I had my ups and downs.
On my very first day at school,
over 60 years ago,
only a mile or two from here,
at the age of five, I ran away.
I ran down the hill and informed my mother
that I did not like school
and that I had no intention of ever returning
(or words to that effect).
My mother, being a sweet and patient lady,
explained that school was something I would enjoy very much
if only I would try it for a little longer.
Of course she was right, and of course I did enjoy it.

Except at certain terrible moments,
such as my tenth birthday,
when I vividly remember being caned (three painful strokes)
for making an unseemly noise during morning assembly.

But as my school career proceeded,
I developed impressive qualities. So much so that I was
given the onerous and responsible position
of tuck-shop assistant, which carried with it
several advantages,
notably an unlimited supply of Maltesers and Crunchie bars.

At the end of my school career, I even became Head Boy,
but I did something that Head Boys
are not really supposed to do.
I led a rebellion against the Headmaster.
I should explain that this was under
the extreme conditions of wartime deprivation.

My rebellion was to protest that we,
the boys, were not getting our due ration of Spam,
a particularly delicious American tinned meat.
Our Spam was being stored in a secret school larder
in case of a German invasion.
I argued that this was most unfair,
and that we should have our Spam *now*.

I was threatened with expulsion,
whereupon I pointed out to the angry Headmaster
that this was rather pointless
as I was leaving anyway in three weeks.
Our Spam was on the refectory table the next day.
But my rebellion was really very polite, non-violent,
and based on reason and justice.

By now, Headmaster, Ladies and Gentlemen, Boys,
you will have gathered that I am not really a suitable person
to give uplifting advice on an occasion such as this.
But I am going to give it nonetheless.

First, I say to all the boys:
you should continually remember how lucky you are.
You go to a very good school,
a school which is better
than many schools to which other boys go.
A school which can help you
to go on later to other good schools.
In being here at Arnold House you are very lucky and very privileged.

But though you are very lucky
and more privileged than many other boys,
you are not *superior* to them.
You simply have a better *opportunity*.
And with that privileged opportunity goes a responsibility,
which is to make the best use of your opportunity, your privilege,
to learn as much as you can about everything,
to develop whatever abilities and talents you may have.
Not just to pass exams, or to be successful later on,
or to make money (though I have no objection to that)
but to be worthwhile members of society,
to be helpful to the less fortunate,
to be considerate and generous to others,
to be of service to the community to which you belong.

But also remember this: though going to a good school
is a marvellous opportunity and a privilege,

it is no guarantee of success or achievement in later life.
The world is full of people
who went to very good schools and have achieved little.
Equally, there are people who did *not* go to famous schools,
did *not* win prizes, and passed few, if any, examinations –
and even became Prime Minister.[1]

What advice dare I give to parents?
As the father of two teenage sons,
I think the best advice I can give
is to succeed where I have failed:
above all, to encourage their sons to read books
instead of watching awful television.
A school, however good, cannot do this on its own.
Parents have a clear duty,
and they should ask themselves
what is the use of spending their money
to send their son to a good school
if he spends all his spare time
watching *Neighbours* or *Blind Date*?
Especially if the parents enjoy it as much as their children.

Finally, may I say this to the boys of Arnold House?
The habit of reading is the most marvellous habit to acquire.
You never forget what you read when you are young.
So read a lot while you are young.
Books about places,
books about people, exciting stories of the past,
exciting stories of the future,
books which will show you the beauties of the English language,
books which excite the mind, and fire the imagination.

Headmaster: a kind viewer wrote to me recently,
"You have now reached the departure lounge of life."
I am only happy my flight has at least been delayed
for me to attend this gathering at Arnold House.

The book of memoirs which I gave as a prize

[1] John Major had become PM three days previously, on November 28th, 1990.

is dedicated to my two sons,
one of whom was at Arnold House.
In the dedication, I urged them to remember
the famous words of the great F E Smith:

> The world continues to offer glittering prizes
> to those who have stout hearts and sharp swords.[1]

---

[1] From the Rectorial Address by Lord Birkenhead (F E Smith) at Glasgow University, November 7th, 1923. By coincidence I had just been born, on October 24th, 1923.

26 70TH BIRTHDAY OF ROY JENKINS

December 12th, 1990, a small dinner party of about 15 people in honour of Roy Jenkins, statesman, biographer and *bon viveur*, on his 70th birthday. The actual anniversary had been a month earlier on November 11th.

The dinner was not grand but civilised and convivial, held in a room at the Garrick Club.

Lord Jenkins of Hillhead had become leader of the Liberal Democrats in the House of Lords. All of us were his friends and admirers, though several of us were not of his political persuasion.

The joint hosts included Lord Cudlipp, Lord Mackie, Sir Peter Parker and Anthony Lester, QC. Also present were Charles Wintour (the former Editor of the *Evening Standard*), author Eric Jacobs, lawyer Ellis Birk, publisher Graham C Greene, and Frank Johnson.

Ian Aitken, the veteran *Guardian* columnist was the chief organiser. He asked me to say a few words. Although the dinner was small and private, it was nonetheless in honour of an eminent parliamentarian and man of letters. I could not hope to equal his eloquence and style. But I did hope to be worthy of the occasion. Afterwards, Roy kindly wrote to me in such glowing terms that I am almost too diffident to quote him, but I do so with permission:

Your speech was spectacularly good – and generous.
I think you are the pre-eminent master of such
commemorative cocktails of warmth and raillery.
I remember you on Ted at the Savoy and on Ludo at
Grosvenor House and I count myself lucky to achieve
inclusion in your gallery.

Gentlemen:

I have been asked to say a few words.
I have reluctantly agreed.
My reluctance is due only to the certain knowledge
that there is nothing I can say
which could not be said with greater authority,
flattery, and blandiloquence
by any of my co-hosts this evening.

Roy, all of us have read your literary works,
we have heard your speeches,
we have seen you rise,
and have seen you fall.

For over 30 years your achievements
and your failures
have been our livelihood,
the raw material for our professional output.

So, this dinner is not merely an excuse
to drink some decent claret;
nor to enjoy some gossip,
pleasures which we have all enjoyed
from time to time in Roy's company –
at East Hendred and elsewhere.

We are here, albeit a little late,
to celebrate his 70th birthday.
In this connection, I must first reveal facts
which are not generally known,
about the circumstances of his birth,
which left a lasting imprint
on his personality and character.

He was born on November 11th, 1920.
As he grew up, year by year,
little Roy noticed with mounting interest
that his birthday was always marked
by a ceremonial 21-gun salute,
and by a solemn silence among those around him in Pontypool.

It was some time before he came painfully to understand
that there was any reason,
other than his birthday,
for the booming guns and the silent homage.
Eventually it was explained to him
that his birthday was also Armistice Day.

Who knows what the subconscious effect
of this was on the young Roy?
I am not much given to pseudo-psychoanalysis of politicians.
I leave that to Dr Anthony Clare or Mr Leo Abse.
But one thing is certain: that in the formative years
of Roy's infancy, these booming birthday guns
and that silent homage
left in him a sense of being unusually important,
a sense which has never deserted him.

But I have never been one of those
who've found Roy lofty, cool and unapproachable.
Nor can I altogether agree with his biographer,
who saw him as the archetypal Balliol man –
"Olympian, enlightened, effortlessly superior,
and with an inability to suffer fools".

A superficial judgement, I think.
Because I can personally testify,
as one of the more prominent fools of my generation,
that he has frequently suffered me,
and he has even appeared to do so gladly.

I cherish a memory of one moment in his career.
This was during the general election of 1983.
I was then a *Panorama* interviewer.
He was then a Prime Minister Designate –
or was it *Joint* Prime Minister Designate?
That *Panorama* interview was unkindly described
by Richard Ingrams as "Woy and Wobin
wambling on about the gwoss national pwoduct".

A kinder critic described us as
"golden oldies of the political scene":

"It was as though Donald Budge and Bunny
Austin had put on an exhibition match on
the centre court."

We, your hosts, are all journalists of one kind or another –
writers, authors, broadcasters.
You, too, have been an author, writer, commentator
and broadcaster,
but unlike any of us, you have also been
a gifted man of government,
a man of great political achievement and action.

Apart from Churchill, no other politician of the front rank
in this century has been as you have been,
not only an outstanding parliamentarian
and a world statesman,
but an accomplished man of letters as well.
Hence it is an honour for us to entertain you.

You were a great reforming Home Secretary.
Some would consider you as the architect
of the permissive society, as the man who opened
the floodgates of filth.
I have always thought that an exaggeration,
because you were not Home Secretary until 1966,
and we all know, if only because Philip Larkin reminds us:

    Sexual intercourse began
    In nineteen sixty-three
    Which was rather late for me.

After the Home Office, you were a highly respected
Chancellor of the Exchequer. You were a leader
in the European Community, who launched the EMS.[1]

You were the deputy leader of an old political party.
You were the founder and leader of a new one.

---

[1] European Monetary System

We remember your parliamentary performances,
notably that in October 1966,
when your devastating speech was even more brilliant
than the escape of George Blake,
which had occasioned the censure motion against you.

We remember the Dimbleby Lecture,
which was to make you the founding father
of the ill-fated Social Democratic Party.
We remember the style and eloquence
which you brought to that and to every occasion.

I have always relished your love
of vivid pictorial metaphor
with which you have decorated your arguments.

In your Dimbleby Lecture, for instance,
referring to Britain's decline you said,
"The Empire has gone with the speed
of soft snow under a warm, damp, westerly wind."

And, deploring the habit of one party
reversing the legislation of the other,
you scornfully declared,
"Spare us too many queasy rides
on the ideological Big Dipper."

But the most ambitious of your metaphors
was in that mould-breaking speech of yours
to the parliamentary press gallery of June 1980,
ten years ago, about that famous experimental plane:

> The experimental plane may well finish
> up a few fields from the end of the runway.
> If that is so, the voluntary occupants will
> only have inflicted bruises or worse upon
> themselves. But the reverse could occur,
> and the experimental plane soar in the sky.

I need not remind this company
that the experimental plane *did* soar in the sky,

but crashed seven years later.
The accident investigators discovered from the black box
that the two pilots had been having an argument.

As journalists, we have all admired
your love of words, your feel for history,
and the felicity of your brilliantly crafted portraits,
such as this, of one of your great predecessors
as Chancellor of Oxford University:

> He was a highly intelligent but
> occasionally ridiculous grandee, a richly
> anecdotal figure, devoted to public
> service, whose strength of character did
> not match his imposing manners and
> appearance.

No prizes for recognizing Lord Curzon. And who is this?

> He was a charismatic vulgarian, a
> visionary who organised thugs, and
> an improbable Wykehamist.

So much for Sir Oswald Mosley.

But your most moving and memorable judgement
was your tribute to your friend and leader, Hugh Gaitskell:

> His memory is a standing contradiction
> to those who wish to believe that only
> men with cold hearts and twisted tongues
> can succeed in politics.

We have admired not only your eloquence but the
physical gestures which have accompanied your oratory.
Such as the one – as if you were unscrewing an obstinate light bulb.
Or, in Frank Johnson's immortal words, as if you were caressing
the breast of a passing duchess.

So full a life have you led,
that in addition to your achievements as parliamentarian,

statesman and author,
you have also found the time and energy to be a social star
in the salons of literary London, and in your clubs:
the Athenaeum, Brooks's, Pratt's,
United Oxford & Cambridge, Reform, and the Beefsteak.
With that list of clubs, a man has almost made it.

This does not mean you have ever been indolent,
though your detractors like to quote you as saying,
"I am a great believer in not working
excessively long hours."

There is a story from the Warrington by-election.
Harold Wilson went up to speak for the Labour candidate,
and against you. He was asked by a mischievous reporter:
"But Lord Wilson, was not Roy Jenkins
a very good Chancellor in your great Labour Government?"
"Oh yes," said Harold. "Roy was a very good Chancellor,
but of course he kept office hours."
Whereupon my old and dear friend Robert Carvel
said, in a loud whisper: "That's the story, boys:
'Wilson too weak to sack lazy Chancellor.'"

To personal criticism and abuse, your response
has always been restrained and dignified.
Asked for reaction to the nickname
bestowed on you by *Private Eye*, you said,
"Smoothiechops is not the name
I would choose for myself, but it does not wound me deeply."

Lastly, Roy: in my opinion, which is not worth very much,
it is a matter of great regret
that you, the eminent parliamentarian,
the biographer of Prime Ministers,
never became Prime Minister yourself.

I wonder how near you were to becoming Prime Minister.
Was there a time, perhaps during
the Wilson '66–'70 Cabinet,
when events might have propelled
you to the very top?

That is one of the questions on which
your forthcoming and keenly awaited memoirs
may, or may not, throw light.

At 70, you are slightly older than myself.
I can't refrain from mentioning what a viewer
said severely in a letter recently to me.
"You are now," she wrote,
"in the departure lounge of life."[1]

I am only happy that my flight, and indeed yours, Roy,
has been delayed long enough for us
to join in this evening's memorial serv...
birthday dinner.

---

[1] Roy refers to this phrase as "starkly memorable" in a footnote on page 565 of his life of Gladstone.

27 SUE MACGREGOR'S 50TH BIRTHDAY

September 16th, 1991, at a large and most agreeable dinner party to celebrate the 50th birthday of Sue MacGregor, the BBC's number one radio broadcaster. Sue was then, as she is still, at the peak of her professional reputation.

The party was in a private house, an immaculate and desirable residence in Denbigh Gardens, Richmond, which had kindly been lent to Sue for the occasion. I had, of course, been to or through Richmond several times, but never to Denbigh Gardens, which was a delightful new experience.

In my five-minute speech I explain, with gentle caricature, the circumstances of my invitation to say "a few appropriate words" at Sue's birthday party in Denbigh Gardens.

The speech and the occasion need one further introduction. An eminent editor who was present praised my "few appropriate words" in terms which were so hyperbolic that his judgement may have been clouded by the abundant hospitality. Hence I will not reveal his name. But he described my remarks as the most touching tribute in a birthday speech that he had ever heard and which almost moved him to tears. As an editor he was not known, I am told, for being lavish with praise.

Ladies and Gentlemen:

Forgive me for this interruption
but, as you've just heard,
I've been instructed
to make the address at this
delightful birthday celebration.

My instructions are to say "a few words",
or rather, "a few *appropriate* words".

But no one has ever been able to rely on me
for words which can be described as *appropriate*.

I should first explain the background
to my presence here tonight.

At a party this summer I ran into Sue.
She was enjoying, as I was, the champagne.

In fact, she appeared to be
rather more affectionate to me
on that occasion than she normally is.

In fact, she seemed decidedly *warm* towards me.
Particularly when she whispered to me,
"What are you doing on August 30th?"

Before I had time to tell her about my plan
to be in Monte Carlo, she said,
"Why don't you join me in my hotel in Amalfi
on the night of my 50th birthday?"

Now, at this point I should reveal
that I have always had two unfulfilled secret ambitions.
One is to have been a popular music-hall star,
such as Des O'Connor or Max Bygraves,
which is irrelevant to this occasion.

But my second unfulfilled secret ambition –
for many years – has been to become
a toyboy, of a celebrated
and glamorous lady of a certain age.

In the words of the song:
"Just a gigolo, everywhere I go."

So, when I received Sue's seductive invitation,
I thought my moment had arrived.

I swung into action,
I cancelled my weekend at Monte Carlo,

I bought some extremely fashionable new beachwear,
I dropped in at Cartier's
to buy her a suitable trinket –
though nothing too exp… vulgar –
as a small token of my affection.

A few days later, I rang Sue.
Ostensibly it was to congratulate her
on the most moving interview she had done
at 6.45 that morning
with the Chairman of the White Fish Authority.

And I happened to add that I was looking forward
eagerly to our night in Amalfi.

But to my bewilderment and consternation,
she said, "On reflection, Robin,
I don't think that hotel in Amalfi is your scene.
I don't think you'd like it."

I pressed her for an explanation
but, alas, none was forthcoming.

However, I did receive a cordial invitation –
not to a romantic hotel room in Amalfi
overlooking the blue Mediterranean,
but to Denbigh Gardens, Richmond, for tonight.

Now, I have nothing against Richmond –
but it is not Amalfi.

So, sadly, all I could do on August 30th
was to ring up Sue at the hotel in Amalfi
(she'd even given me the number)
at 7am on her birthday morning.

And I took great pleasure in telling her
about the contraflow on the M25,
and the milk-lorry which had overturned
at Leighton Buzzard.

This news, I think, got her birthday off to a happy start.

My affection for Sue has grown with the years.
She is one of those unfortunate ladies
whose reputations have been sullied
by their names having been linked with mine
in the gutter press.

I am one of those fortunate men whose reputations
have been enhanced
by that very same linkage.

My relationship with her began
inauspiciously many years ago.
After some BBC party
I took her back to my house.
She seemed a little nervous
so I played one or two of my favourite recordings
which I had usually found suitable
in these situations.

I played one romantic ballad
which I thought would help to relax her.
She jumped and squealed with excitement,
and said, "I remember that one.
My daddy used to sing that to me
when I was a little girl."

Seriously, it is a great delight for me
to be here at this splendid party.

I will say little about Sue's brilliance on the radio
because you all know her to be
a superbly accomplished and well-loved broadcaster.

Her voice is soft and warm.
Her mind is incisive and persistent.
She fondles the microphone
with sensitivity and skill.
She is a mistress of the medium.

She never loses her temper –
not even with Mr Gerald Kaufman.
Though *he* lost *his* with her.

She is the only glittering jewel
left in the BBC's somewhat tarnished crown.

And if, when I am lying in bed at 6.45am,
I *have* to hear about the ugly pile-up
at Newport Pagnell,
there is no one from whom I would rather hear it
than dear Sue.

Happy birthday, Sue.
You don't look anything like 40.
And here is the trinket,
which Cartier would not take back,
to see you into your second half-century.

MY 70TH BIRTHDAY

October 26th, 1993. To the Café Royal for a luncheon to honour me on my 70th birthday. This had been two days earlier, on October 24th.

The luncheon had been arranged by my former BBC colleague John Vernon. One of his charitable activities in retirement was to raise money for the Greater London Fund for the Blind. When he proposed this 70th birthday luncheon for me, for which people would pay to come, I was not keen. I was no longer a front-line peak-hour performer on television. Would many people feel like buying a ticket to have lunch with me? I was very doubtful.

Then John Vernon explained that by consenting to be honoured in this way, I would benefit a most worthy cause, the Fund for the Blind. So there would be a double whammy, to use a phrase which was then not yet in fashion. I agreed. Tickets sold well at £50 and the Blind Fund benefited handsomely. Over 200 people – politicians Michael Heseltine, Kenneth Baker and Jeffrey Archer, colleagues, friends, members of the public, and my elder son, Alexander, aged 19 – sat down for lunch and speeches in the Café Royal. The Chairman was Sir Paul Fox, the doyen of television executives. The two other speakers, who did their best to mock the guest of honour, were Ludovic Kennedy and Chris Chataway, my friends and colleagues since television took off in the mid-'50s.

Mr Chairman:

This event was not my idea.
I was doubtful whether in these hard times
many people would respond to an invitation
to have lunch with me at their expense.

And I feared that if people paid £50
for lunch at the Café Royal
either there'd be precious little for lunch
or there'd be precious little left over for the blind.

"No, no," they said. "Leave it to us."
And I did.

So I am truly overwhelmed
to see you all here this afternoon.
And thank you for coming to this
memorial serv... birthday lunch.

What a glittering company we have:
writers, broadcasters, opinion-formers, doctors,
bankers, academics, TV stars – all human life is here –
pundits, pontificators, parliamentarians,
and ex-future Prime Ministers (I see two or three of these).

In the presence of such a gathering,
I speak with even more than my usual humility.

Thank you, Sir Paul, for saying things
which 30 years ago you never thought
you would ever be saying about me.

Our careers first collided when you became
Editor of *Panorama* in 1961.

In those days, Sir Paul,
you found me a persistent nuisance.
Monday after Monday, week after week,
I would burst into your little office in Lime Grove
and urge you to show flair, nerve and imagination.
And you did – quite often.

I have followed your career with admiration and affection.
So for you to take the chair today
is a great kindness to me.
For you are still the elder statesman of British television,
whereas I am merely an extinct volcano.
My life is moving peacefully towards its close.

Someone else to whom I owe much is here:
the great Sir Geoffrey Cox, former Editor of ITN.
Sir Geoffrey sent me a "small" 70th birthday card

which he has had specially printed for me
to show me how the world looked on the day of my birth.

This is a facsimile reduced in size,
courtesy of the British Museum,
of two now defunct broadsheets,
the *Daily News* and the *Daily Chronicle*
for Wednesday, October 24th, 1923.

The lead story on the *Daily News* front page is as follows:

By Our Political Correspondent

(and I'm not sure whether Sir Geoffrey noticed
these details in the blurred print of the facsimile,
but with the aid of a magnifying glass
I could see what a different world
it was in 1923)

Politicians of all shades of thought
are convinced that a critical phase
has been reached in the career of the PM
and Leader of the Conservative Party.

The PM's intimates assert ...

(no need for a Bernard Ingham in those days)

The PM's intimates assert that he is
being severely pressed by the *wild men*
of the Conservative Party.

Cautious by instinct, the PM has,
on a number of questions,
shown himself responsive to the pressure
of the more robust elements in the Party.

And the Political Correspondent of the *Daily Chronicle*
went on to report that in the Cabinet there was
strong opposition to increases in the burden of taxation.

There have been threats of resignation.
If the PM yields to the wild men,
the Ministerial Party will be smashed
in the constituencies.

The Conservative PM referred to was famously described
as "a man of no experience",
"a man of the utmost insignificance".

That was the verdict in 1923
(sounds like William Rees-Mogg in 1993)
on the pompous Lord Curzon, who had been passed over
by the King in favour of Stanley Baldwin.

Moving on to 1933
(for the only previous birthday which I can recall
with any clarity is my tenth birthday):
on that birthday, in 1933, I was given a short, sharp shock.
I was caned by the Headmaster for a serious offence –
creating a disturbance at morning assembly.

So do not doubt the effectiveness of corporal punishment,
for ever since then, I have never committed
any kind of disturbance anywhere.

The honour for me of this 70th birthday lunch
is highly significant.
It is a signal which shows
that the cult of youth is over.

For too long the young have ruled the roost.
Now the pendulum of popular favour has begun to swing
towards the dinosaurs, towards the *Golden Oldies,*
towards those, like me,
who are riding gracefully into the sunset.

An eloquent protest against "youthism"
has been made by Dr Germaine Greer:
Youthism is the idea that ageing people must give way,
must capitulate, to the young.

Dr Greer speaks for many of us:

> Because others think we are past it [she says]
> we begin to fear that we *are* past it.
> Then we begin to *believe* we're really past it –
> so far past it, that we don't know what *it* is.

Whatever *it* is, I know this:
as I have got older and older,
Cabinet Ministers have got younger and younger.

I was chatting with Mr Michael Portillo,
recently anointed by the Blessed Margaret.
"Mr Portillo, were you ever on *Question Time*
when I was the chairman?"
"I certainly was," said Mr Portillo sharply.
To which I hastily replied, "Of course, of course.
How could I possibly forget?"

And Mr Portillo went on:
"What's more, when I arrived at the studio
I was taken aside by Barbara Maxwell, the producer,
who said, 'Sir Robin is in a filthy temper
because he has never heard of anyone on the panel.'"

Many of my contemporaries and juniors, of course,
are now in positions of power and influence.
I am careful to greet them with politeness and good humour.
I have a standard salutation:
"Still clinging to office, I presume?"
They laugh, because they think I am joking.

But this is no time for frivolity.

As Kenneth Clarke's Budget approaches,
as the Scott inquiry grinds relentlessly on,
and as the Euro-elections loom,
it is not surprising that older members
of the Tory Party are recalling the wise motto
of that veteran back-bencher,
Rear-Admiral Sir Morgan Morgan-Giles:

Pro bono publico, no bloody panico!

I thank Mr Wayne Irving
of the Greater London Fund for the Blind
for organising this lunch.

And John Vernon and Bob Rowland,
old and highly respected BBC colleagues.
I hope the Fund has benefited.

And I thank Chris and Ludo for perjuring themselves.

My thanks to all of you who have come today.
My thanks even more enthusiastically to those
who sent donations without coming to lunch.

You have given me and my son Alexander
(who has the day off from his sixth-form college)
the greatest pleasure.

Daniel, aged 17, is not here.
He is on a study tour of the ruins of ancient Greece.
He says he would much rather be here today
to study the ruins of modern Britain.

As Ludo reminded you,
I have reached the departure lounge of life.

I am only happy that my plane has been delayed
long enough for me to attend
this 70th birthday lunch.

Thank you all very much.

December 7th, 1993. At the Scottish National Portrait Gallery in Edinburgh, to unveil a portrait of Ludovic and Moira Kennedy. This portrait had been specially commissioned by the gallery. The artist was an Israeli, Avigdor Arikha.

Ludo and Moira are two of my oldest friends, from whom I have had over 40 years of kindness, tolerance and hospitality. I am the godfather of their daughter, Fiona Jane.

So when they asked me to do them the favour of unveiling their portrait, I could not refuse – although unveiling portraits is not my speciality. Nor is making a speech in praise of a portrait yet to be unveiled.

It will be noted that I refer to "this brilliant portrait which I have not yet seen". Judging by the artist's reputation, which the gallery assured me was high, I felt no hesitation in calling this portrait "brilliant". I had admired other paintings by Mr Arikha. But when I unveiled the painting, a double portrait of Ludo and Moira together, it was not to my taste. It did not, in my worthless opinion, do justice to this accomplished and glamorous couple, the still glorious redhead Moira Shearer, and her handsome, silver-haired husband. Somehow the painting seemed to make them look awkward. But I have no expertise as an art critic and my comments should be ignored.

At the time of this unveiling, the Scottish newspapers were full of talk about a controversial proposal that the Scottish National Portrait Gallery should be moved from Edinburgh to Glasgow. I was not quite clear why this was mooted, because the gallery in Edinburgh looked fine where it was.

Your Grace, My Lords, Ladies and Gentlemen:

From what I hear, I had better perform my function quickly,
before this painting, and others in this magnificent gallery,
are carted off to Kelvingrove.

But before I do any unveiling,
I wish to say a few words –
although in front of this audience, on this occasion,
I feel lamentably inadequate and out of place.

I am not a Scot. I am not an art connoisseur or expert.
I have no claim to eminence, learning
or distinction in any field whatsoever.

It is true (as the older ones among you may remember)
that I once enjoyed a notoriety from too frequent TV appearances.
Now I am an extinct volcano.

The Scottish National Portrait Gallery
has done me a great honour by inviting me
to unveil this brilliant portrait (which I have not yet seen)
of Ludovic and Moira Kennedy,
with whom I have been friends for nearly 40 years.

The portrait is the work of Avigdor Arikha,
whose previous work for this gallery is greatly admired.

As many of you will know,
Avigdor Arikha is an Israeli who lives in Paris.
He went to Palestine as a boy from Europe at the end of the war.

His life as an artist has not been
a conventional or orthodox experience.
His gift for drawing was first apparent
in the forced labour camps of Eastern Europe in the 1940s.

In Palestine he was wounded fighting
in the Israeli war of independence.

He became an art student in Jerusalem.
Later he set off to study, and then to settle, in Paris.

This is the third portrait which Avigdor Arikha
has painted for this gallery.
The two others are of HM Queen Elizabeth the Queen Mother
and of Lord Home of the Hirsel

(whose portrait is temporarily on loan
to the National Portrait Gallery in London).

And now, today, you have the third in his studies
of Scottish agelessness, Ludovic and Moira Kennedy.

Rarely, if ever, has any artist painted a double portrait
of so beautiful and gifted a couple.

Moira, of course, is one of the great beauties of this century.
You will see in a moment how Avigdor Arikha
has immortalised her on canvas.
She was indeed a challenge to his genius.

By the way, if you have read Ludovic Kennedy's memoirs,
you'll remember *his* portrait (but painted in words)
of Moira, the young prima ballerina
with whom he had fallen in love
after seeing that enchanting film of hers,
The Red Shoes.

"She had," writes Ludo (and I quote),
"the reddest of red hair, a figure like an hourglass,
blue-green eyes the size of saucers, and a most pleasing voice."

Ludo continues, "And if that wasn't enough,
she danced with a grace and lightness
that were breathtaking."

[Stunned silence]

May I have some applause, please, for that?
Not for me, but for Moira,
and for Ludo who wrote those words.

[Loud – nay, fervent – applause]

As for Ludo, he is even more handsome now –
or so I'm told –
than he was in the mid-'50s
when we were colleagues in the early days of ITN.
Today his silver hair gives an impression of wisdom.

But, Ladies and Gentlemen, beauty is not enough,
as I myself discovered during my long
and chequered television career.

Beauty is certainly not the only reason
for their portrait to be hanging here.

They are immensely distinguished Scottish citizens.
Both have reached the heights of their professions.
Both are great Scottish patriots. Not only that:
they are the most eloquent, the most impassioned,
the most committed, the most industrious
and the most indefatigable couple
of communicators and campaigners that I know.

Only last Sunday in my newspaper there was
a scholarly review by Moira of a cellist's biography.

And in the same newspaper,
not one but *seven* expert reviews
by Ludovic of books on naval history,
and on another page a pungent letter
from him to the Editor about euthanasia.

In many causes they are tireless
at a time of life when many people prefer
to grow roses or to sleep in front of the TV.

Ladies and Gentlemen: Ludo has a favourite joke
which I enjoy more every time I hear it,
in which he describes himself
as being "in the departure lounge of life".
Happily his plane has been delayed
long enough for him to see me unveil
this splendid[1] portrait of him and Moira
by Avigdor Arikha.

The people of Scotland can be proud
to have it in their magnificent portrait gallery
here in Edinburgh. I am proud to unveil it.

[1] Which I had not yet seen.

AIDAN CRAWLEY, 1908–1994

February 10th, 1994, St Michael's Church, Chester Square. This was the memorial service for Aidan and Virginia Crawley.

Aidan Crawley, a Buchanesque figure, had given me my first job in television when he was the founding Editor of Independent Television News. He had been a wartime prison-camp escaper, an MP and an early TV star.

His wife was famous as Virginia Cowles, American war correspondent and biographer of Winston Churchill. She had been killed in a car crash in 1983. Aidan survived, badly injured.

At this service I spoke third, after Nigel Nicolson who recalled Virginia in wartime, and Robert Kee who escaped with Aidan from POW camp in 1943. Nicolson and Kee, handsome veterans of World War II, have both in peacetime distinguished themselves as brilliant men of letters. Their addresses were eloquent and moving, and more intimate than mine.

The memorial service was arranged by Harriet, the gifted and lovely daughter of Aidan and Virginia. The church was a few yards from their family home in Chester Square where they had entertained with charm and style for many years.

This beautiful service in memory of Aidan and Virginia
is a celebration for them
and for their brilliant partnership.
They would not have wanted us to be too sad today.

Aidan Crawley was one of my heroes.
He seemed to be everything a real man should be:
ruggedly handsome, tall, athletic,
eloquent, stylish, bold, adventurous.

I had the good fortune to work for him in television.
He became my good friend for nearly 40 years.

When I first got to know him, what impressed me most
were the tales of his prowess as a young cricketer
in the '20s at Oxford.

In the list of those who are recorded
as having hit ten sixes in one innings
of a first-class match, you will see the names
Walter Hammond, Herbert Sutcliffe, Viv Richards, Ian Botham
and Aidan Crawley. There's immortality for you.

Incidentally, when Aidan hit those ten sixes,
he'd just driven sixty miles after dancing all night
at a Commem Ball in Oxford.
A gentleman, you may think, of some style.

Throughout his life, Aidan was a tremendous all-rounder:
sportsman and politician, Fleet Street journalist
and documentary film producer.

Wartime fighter pilot and, as Robert[1]
has so eloquently reminded us, prison-camp escaper.

A Labour MP in 1945, and a Tory MP in 1962.

A writer of biography and an early star of television.

A pioneer of television journalism in the BBC
and the founding father of ITN.

A Minister in the Attlee Government
and President of the MCC.

Who else in our time has lived a life
of such multifarious accomplishment
or displayed such dazzling versatility?

And in each of those different capacities,
Aidan demonstrated the qualities

---

[1] Robert Kee, biographer, historian and TV star.

which characterised his whole life:
courage, leadership, vision, panache.

More than once he felt it right
to resign, in protest and on principle.

As a young journalist in 1936,
he resigned from the *Daily Mail*.
This was because the then Lord Rothermere
had instructed that nothing hostile
was to appear in the *Daily Mail* about
Herr Hitler or Signor Mussolini.

Up with that, Aidan would not put.
For he could see the gathering storm.

Twenty years later he resigned from the Labour Party
because it clung to Clause 4 socialism.
In that, he was 25 years ahead of others
whose names you may recollect.

And in the mid-'50s Aidan resigned as founding Editor
of Independent Television News
because of the ITV contractors' reluctance
to give the infant news company
adequate air-time and adequate money.

Aidan's courage and vision in that crisis
ensured ITN's survival. He had created in ITN
the most important new national organ of news since the war.
ITN went on to revolutionise TV news coverage.
It knocked the BBC news – need I say it – for six.

Some would see the launching of ITN
as Aidan's biggest achievement.
But for him, ITN was only one memorable moment
among many in his long life.
It occupied him for only about one year, and only ten pages
of his 400-page autobiography.

In the '60s, back in Parliament, this time as a Tory,

he advocated radical trade union reform.
In that, he was a Thatcherite long before Thatcherism.

Aidan was so *often* ahead of his time. Perhaps *too* often,
and perhaps too *far* ahead of his time.
That may be one explanation of why,
for all his talents and gifts,
Aidan never climbed higher up Disraeli's greasy pole.

Or perhaps it was because he did so many different things.
He plunged boldly into every experience in life which offered itself.
He moved impulsively and enthusiastically
from one challenge to another.

Whenever he saw a new frontier, Aidan would seek to cross it.
He was a gentleman adventurer, in the best
and most romantic sense of the word.

And, understandably, he called his autobiography
Leap Before You Look.

One obituarist wrote when he died,
"Aidan Crawley could have stepped straight
out of the pages of a John Buchan novel" –
like Richard Hannay or Sandy Arbuthnot.

Throughout his life, Aidan was always hitting out in style,
with bold and spectacular strokes. There were not many mis-hits.

But there was *one* act of stubborn and wilful perversity
for which I am deeply indebted to him:
Aidan gave *me* my very first opportunity
in television as one of ITN's first newscasters.

Even more perversely, he had threatened to resign
if I were not appointed.

I never knew whether his resignation threat
was to demonstrate his independence as Editor,
or to demonstrate his confidence in me.
And I never had the courage to ask him.

His last years were clouded by terrible family tragedy.
When he attended Andrew and Randall's[1]
memorial service in this church, he was very sick and very brave.

He soldiered on, and his six lovely grandchildren,
all here today, gave him great joy.

But he was tired, and towards the end he told his devoted Harriet,
"I have lived too long."

He had lived too long, he felt. But not too long for us.

---

[1] Andrew and Randall Crawley, Aidan's two sons, were killed when their plane crashed in
Switzerland. Their young wives and children were all at this service.

31 OLD SCHOOL CELEBRATION

July 2nd, 1994. To Bembridge in the Isle of Wight for the 75th anniversary of my old school (or one of them). Bembridge School had been founded immediately after World War I in 1919, in reaction against public school orthodoxy, with its military overtones and classical bias.

I did not go to this anniversary with any enthusiasm. Bembridge School (which has since been merged with another school) was very second-rate in my time. Its academic standard was low and it was too small.

But I am grateful for having been taught to be sceptical of our political leaders. At the same time we were taught to revere our parliamentary institutions. So my school-days there were not without value.

And Bembridge School was magnificently situated on the cliffs near Whitecliff Bay. It was a pleasant place to visit. Hence my presence at this 75th anniversary – though there was hardly anyone I could remember well enough to converse with. The trouble with appearing on television for 40 years is that if you go to some reunion, everybody else is liable to know you, but you recognise hardly anyone. This is apt to be a strain.

But on this lovely July day on the cliff tops, boyhood memories surfaced enjoyably and my speech was in the spirit of the evening.

Headmaster, fellow Old Bembridgians:

I'd prefer not to begin by creating trouble,
because that is not in my nature.
But I am not really the right sort of fellow
to speak after this Anniversary Dinner.
I am not a man of any distinction,
or learning or achievement.

I am not worthy to be on the same list of speakers
as, for example, Mr Barry Field,[1]
the Isle of Wight's Member of Parliament –
for the time being.[2]
Or General Sir Peter Whiteley, GCB,
former Commandant of the Royal Marines,
or Sir Richard Parsons, KCMG,
formerly Her Majesty's Ambassador to Budapest,
Madrid and Stockholm – though not all at the same time.

But I can claim a historical connection
with both those eminent personages.
I was an obnoxious and obstreperous boy in Sir Peter's dormitory
when he was a prefect in the Old House in 1938.

And Sir Richard was an obnoxious and obstreperous boy
in *my* dormitory when I was a prefect in 1941.
That was up in Coniston, to which the school was evacuated.

But I am now merely an extinct volcano.
Or, as a kind viewer wrote to me the other day,
"You have reached the departure lounge of life."

Headmaster, I am only glad that my flight
has been delayed long enough for me to attend
this 75th Anniversary Dinner at Bembridge School.

Headmaster, you requested a few reminiscences from us.
You will be glad to know that I have nothing profound
or inspiring to say – unlike previous speakers.
For what I remember most vividly
are small, isolated, trivial incidents,
which flash back to me
as clearly as if it was yesterday.

I recall being fitted for a gas-mask

[1] An undertaker by profession.

[2] No longer.

in September 1938 at the Old House.
I recall, with some shame, making a speech
in a Current History debate
in defence of Neville Chamberlain and the Munich Agreement.

Less portentously, I remember today
a crossword puzzle clue which Tom Stedman had solved.
And what a great schoolmaster Tom was.
[*Loud cheers*] One of the great schoolmasters of the century.
[*Louder cheers*] I am delighted to see his widow is with us.

Tom was sitting at this table in, I think, the winter of 1939–40.
I was sitting next to him
and watching him fill in the 11-letter word.
"That is a good one," I said. "What was the clue?"
He told me what the clue was:
"What the cunning Frenchman said
on the Tuesday of Doncaster Week. Eleven letters."
I, aged 16, had no idea what Doncaster Week was.
Tom Stedman explained, immensely pleased with himself.
The answer was "Legerdemain" – "Leger *demain*"!

And that has remained embedded in my memory ever since,
along with another crossword curiosity of my days at Bembridge:
the fact that "orchestra" is an anagram of "carthorse".
Who can say that one learnt nothing at school!

I remember also saying to Tom Stedman in 1940
what a good thing it was that Winston Churchill
had become Prime Minister, because my father
thought very highly of him. To which Tom snorted,
"Churchill! He's an irresponsible madman."
Which, of course, was the general view of Churchill
among the intelligentsia of that time.

Perhaps the most profound influence on me
at Bembridge was the contemptuous abuse
heaped on our political leaders

---

[1] As the first Headmaster of Bembridge was called.

by the Warden,[1] J Howard Whitehouse, a former MP.
He knew, or had known, many of them personally.
He would say, "The Chancellor of the Exchequer,
d'you see, is an ass."
Or, "The Home Secretary, d'you see, is crack-brained."
Or, "The Minister of Food is a fool, d'you see."
This was very good training for my later years.

Then, finally, there was the incident
of the rebellion which I led when Head Boy.
This was the historic Spam Rebellion of July 1942
at Coniston in the Lake District.
Some of the very old people here at this Dinner
may recall those days of wartime food rationing.
We had ordinary ration books for butter, sugar, meat, etc.
And then there were things called "points",
and once a month the Food Minister ("the Fool")
used to say how many points were needed for dried egg,
or for the American luncheon meat Spam, which was very popular.
You could spend your points how you liked.

But all that spring in the year 1942 at Coniston,
did we see any Spam at all? No.
So I went to see the Warden and I said,
"What about our Spam?"
And he said *our* Spam, bought on *our* points,
was being stored safely in case of emergency,
such as an invasion. And I said, "That's all very well,
but it is the end of term.
Are you then saying that *our* Spam,
from *our* points, to which we have been entitled
for the last few months,
is being held back for others
to eat after we have left school
in some emergency which may never happen?"

At which the Warden blew up
and said he would ask my father
to take me away from the school at once.
I pointed out, with unassailable logic,
that there was not much point in that

because I was leaving anyway
at the end of term in a fortnight.
The tension in the Warden's study was unendurable.
But the next day, and for much of that week,
our tables were full of Spam, glorious Spam.
A fine example, incidentally, of a rebellion
based not on violence but reason.

That is why I have been asked to speak tonight,
not because of my former television notoriety.

Finally, I have a message for the half-dozen
or so people present who, about 55 years ago,
agreed with me here at Bembridge
to meet on the steps of St Paul's Cathedral
at noon on January 1st in the year 2000.
I don't know who any of them were,
but my message is: don't be late!

Headmaster, thank you for your hospitality
and for the magnificent arrangements for this
75th Anniversary Dinner.

LAUNCHING HOWE   32

O ctober 24th, 1994. Hatchards bookshop in Piccadilly, to speak at the launch of someone else's book, which seemed very eccentric. But the author was an old friend and contemporary, Geoffrey Howe, and the book, *Conflict of Loyalty,* was one of the better political autobiographies.

Why was I asked to speak? A good question, which I myself asked. Apparently the publisher wanted to make the book's launch an "event" and different from usual. They may have doubted Geoffrey Howe's capacity to excite the audience. If so, they were wrong. Geoffrey is a quiet but compelling and witty speaker.

The launch was from 6.30 to 8.30. I rose at about 7.15 on the stairs, which made a convenient platform from which to arouse the mob of guests who were crowding in from the street. In fact they kept coming in during my speech. This was highly disconcerting, as was the fact that many guests were wandering about the hidden side areas where books are displayed. Hence they could not see me. I could not see them. All of which was not the most helpful situation for a speaker.

But the atmosphere was terrific. The place was jam-packed with familiar faces from the '70s and '80s, politicians, journalists and the usual book-party-goers.

It was a struggle to get their silent attention and to bring them all into the main area. But we were off, and before too long the audience were enjoying what they had not expected – namely an unpaid review of the book combined with an after-dinner speech before dinner.

My Lords, Ladies and Gentlemen:

I have to ask why am I here at all?
Speeches at a book launch are usually
delivered only by publisher and author –
unless, of course, either of them happens
to have fled the country for some reason.

What then is *my* function this evening?
Am I to be merely the warm-up man
for the serious business of the evening?
In other words, a comic turn to cheer things up?

In which case I am sadly miscast.
For many years I have been a herald of gloom
and disaster, a messenger of misery.
So I'm hardly qualified to raise your spirits.
In any case, I am merely an extinct volcano
or, as someone said as I came in, a dinosaur.

And what a brilliant gathering is here
in this world-famous Hatchards bookshop –
the very bookshop which Lord Longford entered angrily
to protest that his book on humility
had not been displayed in the window –
editors, gossip columnists, critics, broadcasters,
mandarins, opinion-formers, academics,
lawyers, TV stars – all human life is here –
pundits, polemicists, pontificators, parliamentarians,
Privy Counsellors, not to mention ex-future Prime Ministers.
I see two or three of those.

Ladies and Gentlemen: you all imagine you are here
because of this impressively enormous …
enormously impressive book of memoirs.
But the real reason for *my* presence
tonight (unknown to publisher and author)
is that today is my birthday.
I can think of few sleazier ways of celebrating it
than to drink champagne
which someone else has paid for,
especially if it is in honour of my old friend Geoffrey Howe.

And, of course, I am simply here as an old friend,
one who can be relied upon
for what is expected on these occasions –
namely gross flattery of the author.

One thing I am *not* here for is to mention my own memoirs.

And I would not dream of doing so —
except to say that in their handy,
low-price, economy-size, paperback form,
they do make the ideal Christmas present
for someone you don't really like
but can't overlook.

This is not the first launch party
which Geoffrey and I have both attended.
For on February 5th, 1952 (I remember the date well
because it was the night during which
the Queen was to succeed to the throne),
on that night in 1952, Geoffrey and I
were called to the Bar together in Middle Temple Hall,
and wore our barristers' wigs for the first time.

Thus were launched our respective careers.
Geoffrey, of course, was destined to go on
to win the glittering prizes,
and to hold great offices of state.
I, alas, fell by the wayside and rapidly disappeared
into the obscurity of the television studios.

I am certainly not here for political reasons.
I have not been a member of his
or any political party for 35 years – that is, since 1959.

That was, of course, a significant year
in British political history.
1959 was the year Margaret Thatcher succeeded
in entering the House of Commons.
1959 was the year I *failed* to enter the House of Commons.

Such are the quirks of the popular will
by which the destiny of great nations is decided.

From then on, my intercourse with Margaret Thatcher
was only occasional and infrequent.
But Geoffrey Howe served continuously and loyally
under her leadership for 15 tumultuous years.

His partnership with her, he points out,
lasted longer than most marriages.
How came the divorce – and why?
That is only one of the many questions raised
and answered in the 700 pages of this volume,
Conflict of Loyalty.

The title itself, *Conflict of Loyalty,*
is the climactic theme of the book
and echoes the words of Geoffrey's historic speech
in the House of Commons on November 13th, 1990.

No one who heard that resignation speech will forget it.
It was the most dramatic speech,
yet most undramatically delivered,
that I have ever listened to
in the House of Commons.

The only other speech, I think,
which can be compared to it in impact and shock
is one which I did *not* hear –
because I was much too young then
to have a seat in the press gallery –
namely the speech of L S Amery
on May 7th, 1940 in the Norway debate
which led to Chamberlain's downfall.

But for that speech, Amery quoted someone else's words,
the words of Oliver Cromwell in 1653
to the Long Parliament, because it was no longer fit
to conduct the affairs of the nation:

> You have sat too long here for any good
> you have been doing.
> Depart, I say, and let us have done with you.
> In the name of God, go!

There was no such quotation or borrowed flourish

---

[1] Thanks to TV, millions outside the chamber could watch this speech. And future generations will be able to see what Parliament was once like.

in Geoffrey Howe's final sentence on November 13th, 1990.

He concluded *his* argument in his own words,
without raising his voice.
His speech ended with a sentence of cool simplicity,
devoid of rhetoric or grandiloquence:

> The time has come for others to consider their own response
> to the tragic conflict of loyalties
> with which I have myself
> wrestled for perhaps too long.

That, wrote Margaret Thatcher in her memoirs,
"electrified the House of Commons".
It was, she said, an open invitation
to Michael Heseltine to stand against her.

And that quiet speech,
culminating in that softly spoken sentence,
precipitated an event
which had never occurred
in our peacetime history before –
the removal from office of a Prime Minister
in good health whose party has a majority
in the House of Commons.

What kind of a man is the man who chose
to deliver such a fateful message?

Margaret Thatcher summed him up as
"quiet, gentle, but deeply ambitious"
and said she was "exasperated by his
insatiable appetite for compromise".

After reading these revealing memoirs,
you will discover why he, after 15 years
of loyal service to her,
found that his appetite for compromise
had been more than adequately satiated.

You will see the loyalties which were in conflict:

his loyalty to Margaret Thatcher
who was, he says, "beyond argument a great PM",
and loyalty to the true national interest as he saw it.

And if, as you read these memoirs,
questions occur to you, you will find that
the author asks them himself
with characteristic frankness:

What about the big three of the Thatcher cabinet,
Howe, Lawson, Hurd?
Why did they not form a "troika" together
(as indeed the author suggested)
so as to exert more influence
instead of remaining "painfully subordinate"
to the PM's domination?

Should he not have resigned earlier
when she sacked him from the Foreign Office in July 1989?

Why did he then not send in the resignation letter
he had drafted instead of keeping it for these memoirs?

And should he not have stood against her
for the leadership as he was strongly urged to do in 1990
or, earlier, in 1989 instead of leaving it to Sir Anthony Meyer?

These are not *my* questions. They are his, in this book.

Whatever you may think of his answers,
you will perceive the extraordinary qualities
which have characterised his political career.
He is indefatigable. He is imperturbable.

He is patiently tenacious.
He is infuriatingly reasonable.
He displays relentless mastery of complex detail,
and he only needs four hours' sleep a night.

He admits that his tenaciously quiet brand of advocacy
was liable to cause exasperation
in No. 10 Downing Street.

He recalls, "When the crockery stopped flying,
I was still there waiting for the interruption to end."

His sense of humour has style and subtlety.
In his new coat of arms
he takes an elegant swipe at his old adversary,
Denis Healey, who said that being attacked by Geoffrey Howe
was like being savaged by a dead sheep.
For that, Baron Howe of Aberavon has taken heraldic revenge.
His crest on his coat of arms
is a *wolf* in sheep's clothing,
savagely chewing a Red Flag.

I am honoured to have taken part
in this memorial serv… this memorable book launch.

The publication of these memoirs
should not be taken as a signal
that Lord Howe of Aberavon is finished
with politics or public life.

Far from it. At the Bournemouth Conference,
and since, he has been significantly prominent
in the campaign to resist the spread
of what he called "Euroscepticaemia".

He is, of course, still a young man. He is only 67.

Here's to Geoffrey,
with congratulations and best wishes.

33 LAUNCHING COLE

April 4th, 1995, the Atrium, 4 Millbank, Westminster. Another speech at another autobiographical book launch. This time it was for my brilliant colleague, John Cole (he of the overcoat), the former Political Editor of BBC Television. His memoirs were called *As It Seemed to Me*.

Once again, a high-powered company of guests (many of them Old Labour) had an unscheduled diversion, a speech by someone other than the author, which amounted to a gratis in-depth review of his book. Again, as in the case of Geoffrey Howe's book launch, I was surprised to be asked. After all, I thought, John Cole was not only a fine political correspondent, but a great character and a national figure. Surely "Old King Cole" did not need me to crown him.

But apparently the habit of having guest speakers at book launches was catching on. So John asked me and I agreed. We had shared one experience – a heart bypass operation – which we often discussed together.

I was honoured to speak for him. I had admired his work as a political broadcaster and knew of his long newspaper experience. I had furiously sympathised with him during the regrettable period when BBC Television had seemed to be keeping him off screen because of his unpolished Ulster accent. I'm glad to say his memoirs became a best-seller, but not because of my speech in the Atrium of No. 4 Millbank.

My Lords, Ladies and Gentlemen:

I have been asked to say a few words.
I have reluctantly agreed.

But I have an overwhelming sense
of being superfluous and out of place
on this memorable occasion.

A formidable company is gathered here
to launch John Cole's splendid book.
I see parliamentarians, pundits, pontificators,
practitioners of oratory, ex–Prime Ministers,
ex–future Prime Ministers (I see several of those).
So I speak with even more than my usual humility.

What (you may ask) is my function?
I am here simply as an old friend and colleague,
one who can be relied upon
for what is expected at these events,
namely the gross flattery of the author.

One thing I am *not* here for
is to mention my own memoirs.
I would not dream of doing any such thing.
Except to say that in their handy,
cut-price, economy-size, paperback form,
my memoirs are the ideal gift for someone
you don't really like but can't overlook.

We are here for the launch of this impressively enorm…
enormously impressive book of memoirs.

This is not a conventional autobiography or memoirs.
It is sub-titled "*Political* Memoirs".
It is not "inside" John Cole's private life.
It is inside politics.
It is a personal interpretation, from his perspective,
of British politics in the second half of the 20th century
as it seemed to John Cole.

One theme runs throughout:
the fundamental contrast he sees
between two kinds of politics –
not between left and right,
not between Eurosceptic and Eurofanatic,
not between progressive and conservative,
but between the pragmatic and the ideological.

Those two political styles he sees personified

and exemplified in Harold Wilson and Margaret Thatcher.

As to Margaret Thatcher's "addiction to ideology",
he declares a conclusion which (he says)
he would *never* have been free to declare
when he was Political Editor of BBC TV,
that "Lady Thatcher's conviction politics
transformed the tone of British public life,
and not for the better".

For Harold Wilson, John Cole has affection and admiration.
He kept "Britain inside Europe without destroying his party,
through a skill that came close to political genius".

But, as John points out, "there are pragmatists
and ideologues in all parties"
and many politicians (he says)
don't know which they are.

John knows which *he* is. So do I.
He is obviously of the pragmatic tendency
but with a stiff backbone of principle.

What many readers will find most fascinating
are his prejudices and passions
and personal predilections, which he
scrupulously kept hidden from BBC viewers.
He now confesses all and lays it bare for everyone to see.
In this book, the author has "outed" himself!

For who is his "greatest political hero"?
David Lloyd George!
Who is "the man whose attitudes attracted [him]
more than anyone else in politics"?
Tony Crosland.
He confesses (his word) that the man he admired
more than any other Conservative politician he encountered
was – Macleod? Butler? Macmillan? No –
Reggie Maudling, who was the "perfect pragmatist".

John confesses engagingly that he has

"an addiction to flawed heroes"
and explains that he is "a Nonconformist Christian
who does not believe in human perfection".
That's just as well, if you're a political journalist.

On every one of his 436 pages,
there is a sparkling aphorism or anecdote
to illuminate the reader's progress.

There is the story of how Hugh Gaitskell
at one time suspected that John was a Trotskyist.
But later Hugh Gaitskell's suspicion
was much more serious,
"that John Cole was a Wilsonist".

But the story I enjoyed most
was of how Churchill was discussing details
of his state funeral with a young officer
from the Ministry of Defence
(whether the train should go to Paddington, etc).

Sir Winston said:

　　　Now if de Gaulle dies before me,
　　　we will adhere to these plans.
　　　But if I die first,
　　　and de Gaulle comes to *my* funeral,
　　　then my coffin must go via Waterloo.

Ladies and Gentlemen,
some great figures in politics and public life
have a distinctive item of apparel
which the public recognises
and on which the cartoonists seize with relish.

Churchill had his hats and his cigar.
Jo Chamberlain had his orchid and his monocle.
Neville Chamberlain had his umbrella.
Anthony Eden had his Homburg.
Harold Wilson had his pipe.
Margaret Thatcher had her handbag.

John Cole has that glorious garment, his overcoat,
in black and white herringbone Donegal tweed,
which has now been acquired for the nation
by the Victoria and Albert Museum.

We should remember (it seems unbelievable now)
there was a period when some BBC executives,
in their weasel-minded wisdom,
were reluctant to use John Cole on TV.
His Ulster accent, they thought
(perhaps influenced by *Private Eye*), was off-putting
and incomprehensible
to some viewers. Anyone who did think that was wrong,
hondootedly wrong.

Of course, before long,
John Cole was acknowledged not only
as the master journalist which he always was,
but as a natural television performer
who added excitement, personality
and authority to every political moment.

But newspapers were his first and longest love.
He became a reporter at 17,
and was a newspaperman for 36 years.

Kipling might well have had John Cole in mind
when he wrote:

> He hath sold his heart
> To that old black art
> We call the daily press

And that art is displayed in this book
with the brilliance, fairness and humour
which have won him the affection, admiration and trust
of all his colleagues, and of politicians of all parties.

One of the most significant testimonials to him
has come from a politician who is a rival journalist,
the Rt Hon Roy Hattersley, who wrote,

"There is no indiscretion committed by my colleagues
that I would not tell John about."

That says much about John Cole –
it says even more about Roy Hattersley.

My Lords, Ladies and Gentlemen,
I give you a toast:

To John Cole, his book
and to Madge, his wife, who edited out 100,000 words.

34 GUEST OF HONOUR

April 23rd, 1995, Shakespeare's birthday, on which the members of the Garrick Club were holding their Annual Dinner. The origin of the Garrick in 1831 was theatrical and aristocratic. Today the membership is more inclusive. I was elected in 1962, after waiting only four months. Nowadays the waiting list is said to be six years because so many want to become members.

At the Club Annual Dinner, one of its 1,000 members is the Guest of Honour. He has to address a brilliant and potentially critical audience. The Guest of Honour may be a veteran star of his profession. He may have served the Club over the years. He may be a member who, for one reason or another, the Committee judge deserves the honour, which in my case was completely unexpected, and deeply appreciated.

Or it may be (and this is pure speculation) that when I was invited to be Guest of Honour it was because the Committee could not agree on anyone else. Be that as it may, I could not question the judgement of the Committee who are (mostly) men of wisdom.

The atmosphere at a Garrick Club dinner is convivial. The setting is splendid. The silver in the big dining-room gleams in the candlelight. On the dark red walls are hung historic paintings from the golden age (1760–1830) of theatrical portraiture, including, of course, those of David Garrick.

My health was proposed by my great friend Sir Ronald Waterhouse, then the senior High Court judge, to whom I enjoyed referring nostalgically in my reply.

Mr Chairman:

I'd much prefer not to begin by creating trouble
because that is not in my nature.
But I have an overwhelming sense of being an impostor.

When I think of the great Garrick figures

who've been honoured at our Annual Dinners –
the celebrated actor-managers, the legal luminaries,
the literary giants, the matinée idols –
who am *I* to be standing in their shoes?
That is a rhetorical question
which you are not expected to answer.

I am merely a humble seeker after truth –
known derisively in the TV trade as a talking head.

I was much moved by Sir Ronald Waterhouse
for his kind and generous words,
words that would never have crossed his mind,
let alone his lips,
when he and I were called to the Bar together
43 years ago. I remember that night well,
the night that our respective careers were launched.

Ronald went on to win the glittering prizes.
He is now the senior High Court judge.
I, alas, fell by the wayside
and sank into the obscurity of the TV studios.

A few of you may remember the great Donald Wolfit
speaking here at the centenary
of this building in 1964.

"What should *I* say," asked Sir Donald –
speaking (he said) as an "uneducated actor" –
"What should *I* say
to such an assembly of wits and brains?"

That was in 1964, of course.
I know exactly how he felt.
And tonight, I am acutely conscious
of addressing the most daunting
after-dinner audience in London:
practised performers of every kind,
playwrights, publishers,
pundits and polemicists,
parliamentarians and pontificators,

actors and advocates,
editors and entertainers,
critics and columnists,
judges and journalists.

Journalists indeed. Of every quality and calibre:
we have former editors of *The Times,*
and a former editor of the *News of the World.*
Oh yes, all human life is here.

So on this brilliant *fin de siècle* occasion,
I salute the dazzling diversity
of talent, distinction and genius assembled here.

If you think that is over-egging the pudding,
please just look at the member on your left
or on your right.
And if you are not terribly impressed
with either of them, just think of *yourself*
and that should raise your spirits.

I cannot, however, disguise the lamentable fact
that *my* record is one of failure.

I failed at the Bar. I failed in politics.
And any illusions about my career in TV
were crushed the other day by my taxi-driver:
"I do like that *Question Time*
with David Dimbleby on a Thursday night."

I exercised my right of silence
and buried myself in the *Evening Standard.*
But then the driver turned and said:
"Mark you, it's never been the same
since Peter Sissons."

My failure at the Bar cannot be blamed
on my admirable pupil master, Fred Lawton,
later Lord Justice Lawton.
I am deeply indebted to him
not least because he and Sir Geoffrey Cox

proposed me for the Garrick in September 1961.
Fred is now crippled with arthritis,
but in his letters to *The Times* and on the radio,
he still lays down the law as robustly as ever.

Lord Justice Lawton followed my career with mixed feelings,
as he followed the career of another of his pupils,
who also fell by the wayside: Margaret Thatcher.

And talking of her, as I frequently do,
takes me back to 1959.
That was a year of great significance
in British electoral history.
1959 was the year Margaret Thatcher
succeeded in entering Parliament.

1959 was also the year in which I *failed* to enter Parliament.
Such are the quirks of the popular will
by which the destiny of great nations is decided.

I watch with envy and admiration
my friends and contemporaries
who have achieved power and position.
But I am not bitter or resentful.
I give them a genial greeting:
"Still clinging to office, I see."

They laugh. Because they think I'm joking.

Recently I was able to see for the first time
my page in the Candidates' Book.
I deciphered several memorable names
of those who did me the honour of signing it,
names which bring back the Garrick of 1961:

Gerald Barry, Joseph C Harsch, Robert Lusty,
Dingle Foot, Jack Hawkins, Gerard Fay (Stephen's father),
Hugh Gaitskell, Hartley Shawcross – and Donald Wolfit.
Perhaps he was too full of Macbeth
and wanted "to make assurance double sure".
Because he signed my page *twice*!

Another of my supporters was Peter Boydell,
a member of the junior bar,
now, of course, a silk of great eminence,
who told me only the other day
about the Garrick Annual Dinner in 1951.

The Guest of Honour was that legendary master
of the criminal law, Sir Travers Humphreys,[1]
then aged 84 and still sitting.
He turned to young Boydell and casually reminisced:
"As my client Mr Oscar Wilde said to me ..."

Unfortunately, the young Peter Boydell
was so stunned by this name-dropping
that he could not tell me in *1995* what it was
Oscar Wilde did say in *1895*
to his junior counsel, Travers Humphreys.

But I can guess. Because we know
what Oscar Wilde did say to him
when told that the Marquess of Queensberry
had briefed Edward Carson, QC,
who had been a fellow student of Wilde's
at Trinity College, Dublin.

Travers Humphreys explained that Wilde
would be cross-examined by Carson.
Wilde immediately replied,
"No doubt he will perform his task
with all the added bitterness of an old friend."

Many of us have often found that
the conversation here, about new plays and books,
is the next best thing (certainly cheaper)
than going to see the new Ronnie Harwood play
or buying the latest novel by either Amis.

So engrossing is conversation at the Garrick
that the world outside goes by ignored.

[1] Mr Justice Humphreys, 1867–1956.

I remember when the IRA bomb went off at lunchtime
at the Sussex Arms across the road there.
We were all detained on the Club premises.
Eventually I managed to escape through the back
but was accosted in St Martin's Lane by the Press Association.

"Where were you when the bomb went off?"
"I was in the Garrick Club."
"So you heard the explosion, did you?"
"No, nothing at all.
I was listening to Milton Shulman."

Which was faithfully flashed
to the front page of the *Evening Standard*.

For some reason, unlike other clubs,
the Garrick gets itself into the papers
and into debates in the House of Lords.

Recently, Lord Lester – not the *Earl* of Leicester
but Lord Lester of Herne Hill,
our former fellow-member – introduced his Human Rights Bill.

A Labour peer, Lord Cocks of Hartcliffe,
intervened with a mischievous sarcasm
rarely heard in their Lordships' House:

> The noble lord Lord Lester has been in the news recently
> because he resigned from the Garrick Club
> over its admissions policy,
> having, we are told, wrestled with his conscience
> for some 20 years.

Lord Cocks of Hartcliffe continued:

> No doubt, the noble lord Lord Lester
> is clearing the decks
> in order to become politically correct
> in time for this Human Rights Bill.

Whereupon the noble lord, Lord Lester,

hastened to give this assurance:

My bill will not touch the rules
of my former club, the Garrick Club.
Its members can continue freely to exclude women
without being affected by the bill.

According to Michael Charlton,
the purpose of our charming new lift
is to take the club into the 21st century.

Most of us will be content
if the lift, so tastefully decorated in brothel red,
takes us safely up to the bar,
or to the intensive-care unit,
or to the eagerly awaited bedrooms,
provided the rates per hour are reasonable.

Wherever our new lift should take us,
may I be allowed to express one hope
as we approach the millennium?
That we in the Garrick do not fall into a habit
of electing only inoffensive, uncontroversial members.

Let us not have only smooth men
but let us have some hairy men – like Esau, my brother.

Mr Chairman, friends:

I deeply appreciate the honour done me tonight
at this superbly arranged dinner,
especially by that old master
of pictorial defamation, Michael Cummings.

I count myself immensely fortunate
to be among your number.

You may remember, as I do, some affectionate lines
brilliantly composed under the stairs by Kingsley Amis,
to whom I am most grateful:

If spite and envy seek to overwhelm
All humour, all good nature in the realm;
Should dullness try to turn the world to ash,
Here is one place it may find hard to smash;
The last of its opponents to submit,
This citadel of kindness, sense and wit.

Gentlemen, thank you.

35 ITN'S 40TH ANNIVERSARY

September 16th, 1995, in the Great Hall of King's College, Cambridge. This was for the concluding dinner of the annual convention of the Royal Television Society. A reception was held before dinner to mark the 40th anniversary of Independent Television News. ITN and my television career began on the same day, September 22nd, 1955. I was one of ITN's original newscasters.

Many of the convention delegates had left. But at this dinner, on the Saturday night, were all of ITN's editors since 1956 and 200–300 people from the BBC, ITV and associated enterprises.

It was an occasion full of nostalgia for the ITN contingent, including myself. The setting in King's Great Hall was magnificent – infinitely more stately than the familiar banqueting suites of the great London hotels. In fact the academic ambience seemed almost too venerable for the discussion of ITN's short life. But there were some historic events to be mentioned and remembered.

Mr Chairman:

Never in my most ambitious dreams,
did I imagine that an assembly
so distinguished and influential as this
would be gathered in an ancient seat of learning
to celebrate the 40th anniversary
of *my* entry into television.

With your permission, Mr Chairman,
or Mr President – whichever of you is in charge[1]
[*loud laughter*] – or even without your permission,

---

[1] The Chairman of the RTS (Paul Jackson) had called the Loyal Toast after we had already drunk it, as ordered by Michael Grade, President of the RTS.

I shall now call for a show of hands
at this Royal Television Society dinner.

Which of you actually saw the very first ITN bulletin,
transmitted at 10pm on September 22nd, 1955?[1]

That makes me feel like some prehistoric being,
a dinosaur from television's Jurassic age.

Whether you were a viewer that night or not,
September 22nd, 1955 was a climacteric
of Britain's 20th century.
It was the day the BBC monopoly was smashed.
It was the day the viewer had a choice.

Above all, September 22nd, 1955 was the day
that a new national daily organ of news
could challenge the BBC and Fleet Street.
It was the day that workers in broadcasting
had an alternative employer. It was the day
a social and political revolution began in Britain.
Just as now, 40 years later, you are on the verge
of another revolution, this digital revolution.

A less portentous judgement on the events of 1955
was delivered by the veteran TV critic
Maurice Wiggin in the *Sunday Times*:

> Switching over from BBC to ITV
> in those early days left one feeling
> that on the way home from the vicarage
> one had dropped in on a house of ill-fame.

I don't think I was on that night.

It so happens that few of those who lead us today
in television and politics

---

[1] Only four hands were raised.

are old enough to have experienced personally
the coming of competition, especially in TV news.

In September 1955, Mr President,[1]
you were a boy of only 12.
You had not even begun the formative period
of your career, your traineeship on the *Daily Mirror.*

John Major was also only 12.
Virginia Bottomley was seven.
John Birt was only ten, playing happily
with his performance indicators and his attainment targets.
Tony Blair was two.

But no one, however young they are,
should be in any doubt that the creation of ITN
in 1955 was a brilliant landmark
in the history of British journalism and broadcasting.

And ITN steadily grew and flourished –
notably under the editorship,
for 12 critical years, of Sir Geoffrey Cox.
He is now 85,
but I will ask him to stand
so that you may all see
in whose company you have the honour to be.

[*Loud and prolonged cheers*]

[*Sir Geoffrey to RD: "He always gave me trouble."*
RD to Sir Geoffrey: "No heckling!"]

It was he who steered ITN –
when it had only been launched for one year –
through the supreme storm of the post-war period,
the double-barrelled crisis of Suez and Hungary in 1956.

In my opinion, and I am not alone,

---

[1] Michael Grade.

Sir Geoffrey is the greatest television journalist
we have known in Britain.

It was he who laid the foundations
of ITN's 40 years of success and popularity.

He proved, as ITN has proved for 40 years,
that TV journalism does not have to be
tabloid or trivial or yellow to be popular.

It was his achievement that ITN combined
the impartiality and accuracy required by the Television Act,
with the punch and sparkle of Fleet Street.

He was keenly aware that "ITN was not just in journalism
but in show business".

And it was Sir Geoffrey Cox who founded *News at Ten*
in 1967 against stiff opposition from the ITV companies,
thus proving that the public may not know
what they want until they are offered it.

His book, *Pioneering Television News*,
is published on Monday. I commend it to you all.
It is a classic of broadcasting history.
It is a must for all those thousands of students
now flooding into our universities to take Media Studies.

Also at this table tonight are those other editors
who've led ITN through the '70s, '80s and '90s
with courage and flair and enormous professional skill:
Nigel Ryan, Sir David Nicholas, Stewart Purvis.

All of them have borne the editorial responsibility
during dangerous and testing periods.
Not least, for night after night, lest we forget,
during 25 years of bloodshed and bigotry in Ulster.

They and their colleagues have extended ITN's operations
across new frontiers. Especially Sir David Nicholas.
He led ITN for 14 long years.

He launched the hour-long *Channel 4 News*,
which Stewart Purvis led to an outstanding position
in television journalism.
What a triumph *C4 News* has been for ITN!

Now if you think I have exaggerated the difference
which the coming of ITN made,
let me remind you of the ludicrous taboos
and unbelievable restrictions which were swept away
in that post-1955 wind of change.

When ITN started in 1955,
there was an absurd Government diktat –
the "14-day rule", which banned TV discussion
on any issue due to be debated
in Parliament within a fortnight!

You may well say (like Victor Meldrew),
"I don't believe it."
But that was then the rule.
Soon after 1955 it was defied, ignored and dropped.

Don't forget that when ITN was founded,
there had never been any broadcast coverage
of a general election campaign,
not even in BBC news bulletins.
That was so in 1950 and 1955.

In the 1950 election,
a big campaign speech by Churchill,
calling for a summit on nuclear weapons,
was a tremendous worldwide news story.
But the BBC News did not carry it.

"This," wrote an Oxford historian, "was neutrality
carried to the lengths of castration."

So, incredible though it may now seem,
1959 was the first time any general election campaign
had ever been covered on television or radio.

An early hallmark of ITN
was the probing, incisive interview.

Thanks to ITN (this was 35 years
before the Commons was televised)
the people could begin to watch their leaders
being challenged and cross-examined
as never before; soon this became normal.

But it was ITN in its news programmes
which first opened the doors,
and blew a great gust of fresh air
through British broadcasting in the mid-'50s.

In September 1955, less than a quarter of a million homes
were equipped to receive ITV.
The fact that hardly anyone was watching
could well explain why I was ever allowed
to continue as a newscaster.

Mr President, I look forward to being here, again,
at the 50th anniversary of ITN, in 2005.

No doubt we will then be revelling
in the magical multiplicity of digital TV channels.

As to the future of *news* on television,
my personal inclination is that the best way forward
is the rolling, round-the-clock, all-news channel.

But such a channel should not be merely
an endless, meaningless stream of undigested,
unexplained happenings, live and uncut.

That is not real journalism. That's only the raw material.
A glorified *stop-press*. But if we have a truly informative,
comprehensive and entertaining service of news —
not only politics and war —
professionally edited, presented and analysed, around-the-clock,
with pictures, sound and facts in perspective,
now that would be worth having.

A friendly viewer keeps reminding me
that I have reached the departure lounge of life.
I am only happy that my flight
has been delayed long enough for me
to attend this splendid dinner of the Royal Television Society.

I end with the words which you, Mr President,
(when you were Controller of BBC 1)
expressly forbade me to utter at the end of each *Question Time*
(perhaps they were too suggestive, or subversive):

    "Good night. Sleep well."

INTO THE HALL OF FAME

October 26th, 1995. This was a speech at a dinner at the BAFTA headquarters in London. The occasion was the "induction" of myself and two other people into the Royal Television Society's "Hall of Fame". This Hall of Fame has no physical existence. No pictures are hung in it. It is a fairly recent invention (by Bill Cotton, Jnr, I believe) to create another way of giving an award to people who have done well in, or out of, television.

I shared the evening's honour with Carla Lane and Bruce Forsyth. So the awarding committee had chosen a mixed bag. Previous recipients of the honour had included Lord Grade, Alan Whicker and Dame Thora Hird.

Former BBC executive John Gau made a generous eulogy of me. A compilation of film clips (chosen with great skill and humour) covered my 40-year career in six minutes. I then replied.

Mr Chairman:

It is a traumatic ordeal for someone accustomed
to the dismal obscurity of retirement suddenly to be thrust
into the dazzling glare of the Hall of Fame.

For *me* it is a humbling honour
to have as my co-recipients Carla Lane and Bruce Forsyth.

After all, who am I, to be in their company?
That is a rhetorical question which does not expect an answer.

But I must congratulate the Royal Television Society
on the judicious mélange of achievement
which has been selected for tonight's ceremony.
We, the trio who enter the Hall of Fame tonight,

are indeed, to put it as elegantly as I can, a mixed bag:
a brilliant creator of comedy,
an indestructible star of show business, and me –
an ageing warhorse of political battles long ago.

On such an occasion as this,
I would much prefer not to create trouble
because that is not in my nature.
But the generous eulogy so eloquently delivered
by John Gau was a disappointment to me.

When I was invited to be hung in the Hall of Fame,
I did not expect that my 40 years on television
would be remembered for my heavy-handed,
grim-faced interrogations of politicians.
All that – whether in ITN, in *Panorama,*
in nine general elections, in *Question Time* –
all that, I assumed, was now mouldering
in the archival vaults – ephemeral,
long-forgotten and rarely exhumed.

But when I saw my name coupled
with those of Bruce Forsyth and Carla Lane,
I felt that here at last was recognition,
albeit belated, of my contribution
to light entertainment and the merriment of the nation.

The BBC never really understood me.
Year after year, I would ask Bill Cotton
for an orchestra, or even a band,
so I could dance, like Bruce Forsyth,
down the studio steps to conduct a stirring item
on the Exchange Rate Mechanism
or the Common Agricultural Policy.

My secret lifelong dream has always been
to be a music-hall comedian. Nothing sophisticated –
I am just a simple fellow, a Hamlet
who has longed to play the clown.

But, sometimes, that longing has been fulfilled.

You may be surprised to hear
that in the current financial year,
by far the biggest item in my TV earnings
has been from BBC repeat fees
for my unforgettable appearances
in the *Morecambe and Wise Show* 20 years ago,
and shown again at peak time this summer.
That was a defining moment in my career.
They beat me about the head with bottles.

Another high spot which has passed into legend
was my witty interview with Mr Ernie Wise –
which must originally have been scripted
for some wet Saturday night on Clacton pier.

Ernie said to me, "I did not come here to be insulted."
I said to Ernie, "Where do you normally go?"

Then there was my memorable duet
on the *Des O'Connor Show*.
My singing was judged by knowledgeable critics
to be well up to Mr O'Connor's standard.

But my biggest triumph as an entertainer
was during the 1992 general election campaign,
when I was the lead player in a veteran pop group
which caught the public imagination.
The trio who accompanied me in our breakfast-time show
were billed by the BBC as The Elder Statesmen.
But as our run continued,
they acquired various more affectionate names,
such as The Old Devils, The Old Contemptibles,
The Old Codgers, The Old Fogeys,
The Golden Oldies and The Three Amigos.

The critics raved about us.
"Ten minutes of pure mischief," said *The Times*.
According to Milton Shulman, "Their badinage
gave the only glimpse of fun in the election campaign."
Craig Brown lamented, "If only these spats could last for ever."

You may remember the names of my group:
Norman, the Chingford Skinhead, Roy Boy Smoothie Chops,
Denis the Menace or Silly Billy.
What personalities! What performances!
All are now in the House of Lords
and I am in the Hall of Fame.

If I may leave you with the suggestive words
which Michael Grade, your President,
expressly forbade me from using
at the end of each *Question Time*:
Good night. Sleep well!

December 13th, 1995, at the Medico-Legal Society. My address was billed as "Reflections of a Humble Media Man". My subject, when I got to it, was "Why our courts should not be televised". This was shortly after the deplorable circus of the O J Simpson trial, much of which had been seen on British television.

I spoke at the invitation of Judge Arthur Mildon, QC, President of the Medico-Legal Society, a friend and contemporary of mine at Oxford after the war. Judge Mildon had kindly given me freedom to talk about anything I wanted, though he made several suggestions, emphasising that my address should be "entertaining" because we were approaching Christmas.

I had mischievously given my address a deceptive and all-embracing title. This enabled me to reminisce, not too seriously, about my television career before I came to my theme: the argument against having TV cameras in court.

This address to the Medico-Legal Society presented for the first (and still, so far as I know, the only) detailed and thorough case against courtroom TV – a case which, to me, is overwhelming.

The audience were surprised. They had not known what to expect, and they had not expected me to say what I did say. This may have made my argument more entertaining to hear.

Mr President:

I have an overwhelming sense
of being the wrong man for this occasion.
Here am I, appearing before a learned audience
which is accustomed to being addressed
by speakers of great eminence from your professions
on such recondite subjects as (I see from your programme)
corporate manslaughter, keyhole surgery and sado-masochism.

After all, who am I? (That is a rhetorical question,
which does not expect an answer.)

I have no learning or scholarship or distinction.
For many years I have been only
a humble seeker after truth.
If you think I am joking, just look at Mr Jeremy Paxman,
or listen to Mr John Humphreys,
and you will realise that I am the last survivor
of the age of deference.

I am lamentably ignorant about medicine or surgery,
though I did once lecture to a seminar
of cardiologists at Gleneagles Hotel
about my multiple heart bypass operation.
About which, of course, I knew nothing
because I was unconscious at the time.

I do know a bit about the law.
A year or so as a pupil barrister
gave me an above-average understanding
of how our system of justice works.
More recently, in the 1970s, I spent four years
as a member of the Phillimore Committee
on the Law of Contempt of Court.
I mention that only to tell you with smug satisfaction
that we recommended (in 1974) an inquiry
into the grave dangers of cheque-book journalism,
the offering of money to witnesses,
and into the need for legislation
to restrain or prevent this practice.
Our recommendation was ignored.
No such inquiry was carried out.
But now, following the trial of Rosemary West,
the Attorney-General is carrying out that inquiry
which our committee recommended 20 years ago.

My main reason for feeling inadequate
is your instructions, Mr President.
You expected (you said in your note) an address which should be
"far-ranging, provocative, informative, instructive,
nostalgic, anecdotal and (having regard to the season of the year)
entertaining". You don't want much, do you, Mr President!
Entertaining? Me? I am not some Christmas-time comedian.

Far from it. I am not one of those broadcasters
who've brought happiness into your hearts
or laughter into your homes.
For 40 years I have been a messenger of misery,
a herald of conflict and gloom.

Some of you may be old enough to remember my past:
I was an interviewer on the BBC.
For nearly 30 years I worked for a programme called *Panorama*.

I often interviewed Margaret Thatcher – without much success,
notably at the general election of 1987,
when she was in full flow and unstoppable.
At one point I was driven to suggest,
with the greatest respect, of course,
that an interview must depend on the interviewer
asking some questions occasionally.
According to the *Daily Telegraph* critic,
"Sir Robin was crushed with the effortlessness
of a beautifully coiffured steam-roller."

So I don't have much to be nostalgic about in my career.
Unlike yours, Mr President, mine has been downhill all the way.
You, sir, celebrated at Oxford for your gift of the g…
your great eloquence, you were clearly destined
for the glittering prizes which you duly won:
a lucrative practice at the Bar, silk, a judgeship,
and not least President of the Medico-Legal Society.
Whereas I, having been called to the Bar, soon fell by the wayside
and sank into the obscurity of the TV studios.

I first entered TV 40 years ago.
That makes me feel like some prehistoric being –
a dinosaur from television's Jurassic age.
Then there was no colour, no videotape, no electronic news gathering,
no computerisation, no high-tech graphics, no satellites
to bring you instant reports from any war
or assassination anywhere in the world.

Now we are on the brink of an even bigger revolution,
the "digital" revolution, with the prospect

of a magical multiplicity of new channels.
This will mean new frontiers for TV to cross,
and new territories for TV to invade.
Television has always sought to occupy new territory –
often to the great benefit of a mature democracy.
I take some pride in having been the earliest campaigner,
as long ago as 1959, for televising Parliament.
At first there was deep-rooted hostility.
But eventually the cameras were admitted by the Commons –
as an experiment – in 1990.
They are now accepted at Westminster and taken for granted.

But whereas I have always been totally convinced
that it was right to televise Parliament,
I am equally convinced that it would be wrong
to televise our courts of justice.
But is that a serious possibility?
How near are we to going down the American road?
I would like to offer some reflections on that question.

For several years, television in British courts
has been seriously considered and investigated.
The O J Simpson trial in Los Angeles
may have turned many of us against
the thought of cameras in the Old Bailey.
But TV still has its advocates, even in the legal profession.

The basic argument for letting TV into the courts
can be simply stated: trials are of public importance and of public interest.
The public has a right to be clearly
and fairly informed about what happens in court.
TV is now the main source of news for most of the people.
If the public is not allowed to see
on their television what goes on in court,
how, in the late 20th century, can justice be seen to be done?

This argument has won significant support.
In 1989 a working party of barristers led by Jonathan Caplan, QC,
set up by the Bar Council, unanimously concluded
that the televising of English courts should be permitted on an
experimental basis.

And last year, BBC TV transmitted experimental coverage
of criminal trials in Scotland.
This historic experiment was with the approval
of the senior Scottish judiciary.
These programmes were documentary-style,
recorded and transmitted some time after the trials,
with no news coverage or "live" broadcasts.
It was a limited experiment and carefully controlled.
It was no real guide to anything which could happen
if cameras were regularly in court
for "live" and urgent news coverage of sensational trials.

Then came the extraordinary O J Simpson trial in LA.
Some of it was seen "live" on British screens night after night.
That stirred up a new debate in Britain
about whether trials should be televised here.
That OJ trial was a deplorable circus for many reasons –
the behaviour of the lawyers inside
and outside the court, the race issue,
the Los Angeles Police Department,
the American constitution which puts a free press
above a fair trial, the failure of Judge Ito
to control his court adequately.
But all these problems and difficulties
were intensified and magnified
by the presence of the TV camera,
and by the awareness in that LA courtroom
of the huge audience at home.

There have been conflicting reactions
to the OJ trial in this country.
Lord Browne-Wilkinson, a Lord of Appeal, declared:

> The O J Simpson trial has cast a blight on televising the courts
> and it has changed my own opinion, which used to be in favour.
> It shows that lawyers who are supposedly dealing
> with a case in court are distracted
> by playing to the cameras in a quite disgraceful way.
> This does not lead to the fair administration of justice ...
> The O J Simpson case became an obscene jamboree.

But Mr Anthony Scrivener, QC, former Chairman of the Bar,
said (during the O J Simpson case)
that he *supported* TV coverage of our courts.
And he went further, in words which I noted down
with incredulity. He asserted that "the vast majority
of judges would not mind TV in their courts".

No doubt Mr Scrivener knows more judges than I,
but I respectfully beg leave to doubt
whether most, or many, of our judges
are in favour of admitting television.

The Chief Constable of Sussex, Mr Paul Whitehouse,
came out strongly *for* TV:

> Justice has not only to be done
> but has to be seen to be done,
> and the way to achieve this
> in the late 20th century is to let television into the courts …
> It would educate the public and at the same time
> demonstrate the shortcomings of the legal process,
> thus helping to generate reform.

However, the Chief Constable admitted that:

> There is a danger that only the more sensational trials
> would be covered, such as that of Rosemary West.

That is not just a danger, but a certainty.
TV's appetite for the sensational and the salacious is insatiable.

Is it not a sickening and shocking thought
that a trial like that of Rosemary West
might be watched in millions of homes
if TV were allowed into our courts?
There will be other cases that are horrific and gruesome,
and whose sexual details have a hypnotic effect.
Make no mistake about it: that is the sort of trial
which TV would want to cover,
whatever we may be smoothly told
about the educational intention of the coverage.

The broadcasters (eg the BBC and ITN)
gave evidence to the Caplan committee that they were "keen"
(John Birt's word) to televise the courts.
There would be edited news reports,
and late-night summaries during trials of public interest,
and trial coverage could be used
in documentary, educational and specialised programmes.

It was clear (says the Caplan report)
that the material used would invariably be recorded and edited.
"Very rarely" would there be "live" coverage.
If that reassures *you*, it does not reassure *me*.
I have no doubt that TV would press
for "live" coverage of sensational trials
and that this would happen more and more, not "very rarely".

And if most trial coverage is to be edited,
could TV give a fair and accurate report?
What would we see in "edited news reports"?
We would see clipped from the day's recordings
the most newsworthy moments, the juicy bits,
a witness breaking down,
a gruesome exhibit, a clash between counsel.

Editing, of course, would be professional, skilful and dramatic –
like the highlights of a test match,
when every ball either takes a wicket
or goes for a boundary.
But would we ever see a cross-examination in full,
or get a fair impression of evidence given by a witness?
Not, I think, if we had only edited highlights.
But if the TV coverage is "live" and continuous,
as in the OJ trial as seen in the United States,
the camera with its mass audience is liable
to turn the judicial process into entertainment.

To put it even more bluntly, as one American observer wrote:

> By permitting cameras in the courtroom,
> Judge Ito instantly destroyed any hope
> that O J Simpson, let alone Nicole Brown Simpson

and Ron Goldman, would receive a dignified and balanced hearing.

Commenting on the OJ trial, Mr Jonathan Caplan, QC,
Chairman of the Bar working party (1989),
maintained that in Britain there would not be a media circus
because of our contempt-of-court rules
which would apply to TV as they do now to newspapers.
And Mr Caplan added, "The judge could kick out the cameras
at any time if he decided they were not
in the interest of justice."
That sounds very reassuring,
but once TV was routinely established in court,
how often would the cameras be "kicked out" in practice?
Would not the judge's action in so doing
be seen as highly controversial and provoke strong protest?

What of the argument that TV is primarily an "entertainment" medium,
and would degrade the dignity of the judicial process?
The Bar working party, chaired by Mr Caplan, QC,
dismissed this in their 1989 report
as a "purely emotive and misconceived view of TV".
Entertainment, argued Mr Caplan's working party,
is only *one* function of television,
which also has educative and informative functions.
Church services, they pointed out, are not trivialised
by being broadcast on TV. Indeed not.

There are certainly many examples,
from the Coronation onwards,
of solemn and sacred events being brilliantly televised
without being trivialised or vulgarised.
But a criminal trial is not a ceremony.
It is not a religious service. It is not a show.
It is not staged as a spectacle. It is not an event
designed to arouse fervour, emotion or excitement.

Of course, a trial in court may prove to be moving
and exciting, or even entertaining, but that is not its purpose.
A trial may well be dramatic but a court of law is not a theatre.
A trial is intended to be a cool, impartial and unemotional hearing
of evidence before a judge and jury.

Its purpose is not to entertain
but to establish whether a criminal charge
has been proved against the accused beyond reasonable doubt.

A N Wilson of the *Evening Standard*
sat through every dreadful day of the Rosemary West trial.
He noted with much admiration what he called
"the conscious lack of emotionalism
with which the trial was conducted".

And Mr Justice Mantell, who conducted the West trial,
warned the jury as follows in the summing up:

> Resist external voices which massive publicity
> is capable of bringing to bear.
> Put aside all prejudice and sentiment.
> Cool heads are needed.

If TV cameras were in court, would not the "external voices
brought to bear by massive publicity"
be infinitely louder and harder to resist?
Would not TV encourage (in other words) hysterical
and prejudiced mob reaction to verdicts or sentences?

We should, therefore, before allowing cameras into court,
be satisfied that television, in adding
its mass-audience dimension, would not impair
the dignified administration of justice,
nor destroy the calm, rational atmosphere
in which a trial should be conducted.
We should learn the lessons of the American experience.

But was the OJ "circus" really relevant to British conditions?
Are we in Britain not able to ensure that *televised* justice here
could also be *civilised* justice?
We take pride in our legal tradition,
in the integrity and high quality of our Bench and Bar.
They have Judge Ito, we have Judge Mildon.
We have strict contempt-of court-rules
to protect fairness of the trial.
We rightly insist that press freedom

should not include freedom to prejudice a fair trial.

All true, if somewhat complacent.
Unfortunately, the dangers inherent in TV coverage of courts
would not be overcome merely
by the different nature of our judicial system.
The behaviour of advocates, even of judges, even Judge Mildon,
could still be influenced by the camera and by its mass audience.
Witnesses would still suffer the camera's ruthless exposure.
Consider the effect of TV exposure
on an accused person who was found not guilty.
He may have been seen giving evidence for several hours or longer.
When he leaves the court a free man,
his face would be familiar to millions after a televised trial.

Another danger is that TV coverage,
especially if it is "live", could encourage witnesses
to blurt out irrelevant, scurrilous and defamatory rubbish
in the witness box, where evidence is absolutely privileged.

What of the basic argument that TV is entitled,
at the end of the 20th century,
to the same rights as the press to report trials?
But TV does not merely transmit pictures of the proceedings.
The TV camera is liable to affect the manner
and demeanour of the person being televised,
be that person a judge, an advocate or a witness.
The presence of a TV camera would add appreciably
to the stress and strain of being a witness.[1]
This could affect the reliability of the evidence.

TV coverage cannot be simply equated with press reporting.
TV would not show witnesses if this would endanger their safety.
Again, TV could never show the jury.
That was so in the OJ trial, and in the BBC Scottish experiment.
TV could thus show only part of the trial scene.
TV's part would be more vivid,
but press reporting of the whole would be more balanced.

[1] The British au pair Louise Woodward, speaking at the 1998 Edinburgh TV Festival, complained of this.

What, you may ask, is the difference in principle
between televising Parliament, for which I persistently campaigned,
and televising the courts of justice?
First, there is only one Parliament[1] – the prime forum of national debate.
There are dozens of courts, hundreds of trials.
TV would choose which trials to cover.
Those involved in the trials which the cameras happened to cover
would suffer the extra ordeal of exposure to TV.

Second, MPs are in Parliament of their own free will.
They are there because they asked people to elect them.
In criminal trials, those involved, such as the accused or witnesses,
have no option but to attend.

Third, MPs are long accustomed to performing.
TV cameras have made their behaviour no different
from that which it has always been.
But in a televised trial, the camera would influence
and change the behaviour of those involved,
whether lawyers, judges or witnesses.

Last, Parliament historically is a theatre as well as a workshop.
It is right for TV to transmit the theatre of Parliament
with the humour and the drama of debate.
But a court of law is for calm and dispassionate enquiry.
The liberty of an individual may be at stake.
A criminal trial is not for mass entertainment.

Whatever may seem to be contemporary, modern, fashionable
or correct, let us not inflict TV on our courts.
One American legal commentator said after the OJ trial:

> The TV cameras have turned the dispassionate search for justice
> into a spectator sport, for the amusement
> of drooling couch potatoes.

38 SIR RONALD'S 70TH

May 8th, 1996. Brooks's Club to propose the health of Sir Ronald Waterhouse on his 70th birthday. Sir Ronald's name has appeared quite often[1] in this collection of celebratory speeches.

We were called to the Bar on the same night in the Middle Temple. When he was a barrister in 1955, he rang me at Broadcasting House to tell me of the ITN advertisement for newscasters, which was the start of my TV career. This 70th birthday party was also to mark his retirement as the senior High Court judge after 18 years on the bench.

The audience in Brooks's Club was select, and learned in the law. Eminent judges and silks were present. Clearly this was an occasion when words needed to be well and carefully chosen. And brevity was desirable before an audience most of whom were either experts in advocacy, or whose judicial life involved listening to advocates speaking often at a greater length than necessary.

Since his retirement, Sir Ronald has been given a major judicial responsibility. He was appointed to be Chairman of a tribunal (under the 1921 Act) to inquire into child abuse in North Wales.

My Lords, Ladies & Gentlemen:

On this, the 70th birthday of Sir Ronald Waterhouse,
I do not wish to create any trouble – because that is not in my nature.
But I have been given two contradictory instructions:
one is to propose a toast, the other is not to make a speech.
How I obey the former without *dis*obeying the latter
has not been explained to me.

In any event, in the presence of this formidably learned

---

[1] See also Speeches 12, 22, 34, 43.

and distinguished audience, I feel lamentably inadequate for my task.
Rarely has so much eloquence and eminence,
or such wisdom and wit, been assembled in one room.
Why, indeed, do I have the honour of proposing this toast?
As one of my oldest and closest friends,
Ronald knows he can safely rely on me
for what is required on these occasions,
namely the gross flattery of the toastee by the toaster.

Seriously, Ronald, as you enter your eighth decade,
the years lie well upon you.
Though several people, looking at us both, have expressed surprise,
nay disbelief, that *you* are younger than I am.

Ronald and I were called to the Bar together
44 years ago in the Middle Temple.
It happened the night during which HM the Queen
succeeded her father to the throne.
We both remember the date very well – February 6th, 1952.

Thereafter, with steady brilliance, Ronald went on
to win the glittering prizes of his profession.
I, alas, soon fell by the wayside and disappeared
into the flickering obscurity of the television studios.
I have followed his career with increasing admiration.
This occasion enables us not only to celebrate his 70th birthday
but to regret that he has now retired as the senior High Court judge.
And, moreover, to regret that he has decided to retire so early.
For constitutionally he could continue until his 75th birthday,
whether the government liked it or not.

You will realise what a long time ago it was
that he became a High Court judge
when I remind you that Ronald was appointed
by a Lord Chancellor in a *Labour* government.
Eighteen years on the High Court Bench he feels is enough.
So he decided not to serve his full sentence.

As we mark this culmination of his long career in the law,
the less said the better about his earlier years at the Bar,
though he would not want me to be economical with the truth.

As a young barrister, Ronald was the libel lawyer for *Private Eye*.
You may well be surprised to hear
that *Private Eye* ever bothered to have a libel lawyer.

Ronald has been no narrow specialist in the law.
The length and breadth of his experience
is matched by few, if any, of our senior judiciary.
Thirty years ago this month, he was one of the prosecuting counsel
in the dreadful Moors Murders trial.
Later he was nominated by the Attorney General
to be counsel to the tribunal
set up by Parliament to inquire into the 144 deaths
(116 of them children, mostly under ten) in the tragedy at Aberfan.
During his years on the Bench,
Ronald has figured in many a colourful *cause célèbre*:
a *Coronation Street* libel one day, the trial of Ken Dodd the next.
But I must not anticipate his memoirs.

I am delighted to pay this tribute to him
because Her Majesty's judges don't get much praise nowadays.
In fact, they are the targets of scurrilous abuse from politicians,
tabloid editors, cabinet ministers and television pundits.
Only last week, a notorious columnist in the *Daily Mail*
went so far as to say this, and I quote:

> Barely a day goes by without some bewigged buffoon
> delivering a judgement which makes the courts
> seem to be in the grip of a collective madness.

Only my natural good taste and restraint prevent me from revealing
which "bewigged buffoon" the columnist had in mind, but of course
there was *no* reference, expressed or implied, to Mr Justice Waterhouse.

Ronald may seem to some of you to be
a sophisticated, stylish, metropolitan figure.
But in reality he is a simple, unspoilt fellow
from the Welsh hills, or valleys.
He comes of good radical stock. Indeed, his father knew Lloyd George.
But a member of the family assures me that his mother did not.

No friend of mind has been more generous,
more courteous, more candid, more good-humoured,
more warm-hearted or more infuriatingly distinguished.

Dear Sarah, thank you for inviting us to this splendid party.

I give you all a toast: Happy birthday, Ronald.

39 SIR EDWARD HEATH'S 80TH

July 18th, 1996, the Savoy Hotel, to be one of six people speaking in honour of Sir Edward Heath's 80th birthday. The other speakers were Kenneth Clarke (who was first, and best, and without notes) and Roy Jenkins, Denis Healey, David Hunt and Michael Heseltine.

I spoke fifth, after Hunt and before Heseltine. By the time (well after 11pm) that I rose, things were running an hour or so late. Celebration banquets for several hundred people do tend to be slow. And some of the speakers spoke at party conference length. But it was a splendid evening, covered exclusively by *Hello!* magazine.

Sir Edward was resplendent in a white tuxedo, as was I. We both looked like 1940s dance-band leaders.

There to honour him were his fellow elder statesmen, from all political parties. And the guests included eminent non-political figures – from the world of music, for instance, such as Maestro Rostropovich.

It was an eminently civilised occasion, except that the speakers, who were asked to speak for two minutes, spoke for much longer, except for me. I did as I was told. By the time I rose the audience was beginning to tire of birthday oratory, so brevity was best.

Though Sir Edward did not finish his speech till after midnight, he enjoyed himself enormously.

Sir Edward:

It may well be asked, as we approach the midnight hour,
what am I doing here in this august procession
of the great, and the good, and the golden oldies,
not to mention the Balliol men.
I am nothing but a humble seeker after truth –
the last survivor of the Age of Deference.

I am here because it was my privilege
(and it *was* a privilege) to cross swords on television
with Ted at critical moments of his career,
moments of victory and triumph, of defeat and frustration.
But he never bore me the slightest ill-will.
At least that's what I thought, until one warm, sleepy afternoon
at the Königswinter Conference in '79.
Suddenly up stood Ted to cut through the waffle
and to make his first utterance since losing the Tory leadership:

> I just want to explain why political leaders
> lose elections and get kicked out of office.
> The reason is ... *[by now we were awake]*
> the reason is that the people get bored
> by seeing the politicians interviewed so often
> by the same boring interviewers.
> I have never understood why,
> instead of getting rid of the boring politicians,
> we don't get rid of the boring interv...

I regret to say the remainder of his words
was drowned in loud and prolonged applause.

One of Ted's most attractive qualities
is his macabre sense of humour.
You never know whether he is being funny or not.

Which reminds me of the 1970 general election.
The BBC had a ridiculous programme called *Election Forum*.
Questions were sent in from voters to put to the party leaders.
Flicking through the thousands of postcards
for a question out of the ordinary,
I suddenly realised I held in my hand electoral dynamite.
A postcard addressed in youthful handwriting
to the Rt Hon E Heath, Leader of the Conservative Party,
c/o BBC, Lime Grove, W12.
This question read as follows:

> Dear Daddy,
> When you get to No. 10, will you do
> the decent thing and have Mummy and me to tea?

What was I to do? Should we use it or not?
Here was the key to a general election.
I remembered what Disraeli said
when he heard about some escapade of Lord Palmerston:
"For God's sake keep it quiet or he'll sweep the country."
I consulted a wiser man than I. "Of course you must use it,"
he said, "but only in rehearsal." So I did.
Ted's response can now be revealed.
His shoulders shook with silent, noncommittal mirth.

But this is no time for flippancy.
As Ted enters his ninth decade, the skies are darkening.
A general election looms closer.

  Nearer and nearer draws the time,
  The time that shall surely be ...

Indeed, Ted has felt it necessary to warn that in Canada
the Conservative Party was reduced to two MPs.
What worries Ted if that happens here
is, "Who would be the other one?"

This has been a fine memorial serv... birthday celebration.
Congratulations, Ted. May you continue to say what you think,
without fear or favour, for years to come,
from your corner seat below the gangway.

Many happy returns.[1]

THE OXFORD UNION'S 175TH

40

F ebruary 19th, 1998, at the Oxford Union to be one of eight visiting speakers in the society's 175th anniversary debate. The motion: "Ambition is the last refuge of the failure". The Oxford Union was founded in 1823. The young Gladstone was President in 1830. Ever since then it has been a place where undergraduates practise debating in the parliamentary manner, and try to become persuasive and entertaining speakers.

Nowadays the Oxford Union is said not to be what it was. It never has been what it was. And it never was what it is too often said to have been. But many political figures got a lot out of it when they were young. Five Prime Ministers began their politics here: Gladstone, Salisbury, Asquith, Macmillan and Heath. Other Union stars have been F E Smith, Sir John Simon, Lord Curzon, Sir Walter Monckton, Lord Hailsham, Michael Foot, Roy Jenkins, Anthony Crosland, Tony Wedgwood Benn, Michael Heseltine, William Hague, Benazir Bhutto, Peter Jay, Paul Foot and Brian Walden.

That list does not suggest that there is a single "Oxford Union style" of speaking. There is not. But one of its traditions is the speech which has more style than substance, more elegance than eloquence. This is the style favoured in end–of–term debates and in this 175th anniversary debate.

The eight visiting speakers – far too many – were Michael Beloff, QC, President of Trinity College, Sir Patrick (now Lord) Mayhew, Kenneth (now Lord) Baker, Lord Beloff, Peter Jay, Boris Johnson, Jeffrey Archer and myself. All of us had been President or had held office in the Union except for Lord Archer.

The Union debating hall, with its busts and portraits of statesmen on its walls, was packed to overflowing, with many seated on the floor or standing. It was an audience which any speaker would relish – enthusiastic, responsive and quick on the uptake.

The great virtue of this debate, which will give it a memorable place in the Union's history, was that the eight speakers between them spanned over half a century, going back to 1935. Each

speaker displayed a different style, the style of his time. The best was
Lord Beloff, aged 84, who spoke brilliantly without notes.

My effort got a good reception, much to my relief. You never
know what undergraduates will find funny.

The President was Clare Dixon of St Anne's.

It is, Madam President, a great pleasure for me
to support the President of Trinity[1]
in moving this important motion on which so much depends
and which has just been opposed[2] with irresponsible flippancy.

It gives me even greater pleasure
to see here his father, Lord Beloff,
because he spoke brilliantly from this despatch box
at my invitation in the summer of 1950.

But Lord Beloff's memory of this Society
goes back much further than that:
66 years ago Mr Max Beloff, Corpus Christi College,
was a Teller (he counted the ayes)
at the most famous and notorious debate
in the Union's 175-year history,
the King and Country debate of February 9th, 1933.

That little detail of history may seem irrelevant,
but at least it reminds the other speakers
(like me) how young we really are.

Your letter of invitation to *me*, Madam President,
expressed flattering confidence in my debating ability:
"I don't think it will make much difference
which side you speak on."

It is clear that we, the speakers, have only one duty:
the gross flattery of yourself, Madam President.

[1] Michael Beloff, QC.

[2] By Lord (Kenneth) Baker of Dorking, CH.

Your historic term of office has so far,
you tell me, been brilliantly successful.
You are presiding over these anniversary events
with eloquence and elegance.

Forty-eight years ago, when I had the honour to occupy your chair,
one of my duties in those prehistoric days
was to write a critical review of each debate.
Among the speakers whom I noted as being "very able"
was a Mr Gerald Kaufman of the Queen's College.
He "expressed a socialist's contempt
for the Labour government".
(Nothing changes much, does it?)

I delicately reported that a Mr William Rees-Mogg (Balliol)
had just made a "thoughtful speech
which improved as it proceeded".
(Which was just as well, I can tell you.)

Then I noted another promising fellow, a Mr Patrick Mayhew (Balliol)
who "rolled out picturesque metaphors
in an impressive voice". Which he has gone on doing ever since.

Tonight I am sad to see no undergraduate speakers on the paper.
I came here expecting to cross swords
with Oxford's gilded *youth*, with the great leaders of tomorrow,
with the future William Hagues.
What do we have instead?
A bunch of middle-aged Establishment grandees!
And, worst of all, *me*. Why on earth have *me*?
Who, after all, am *I*?
That is a rhetorical question which does not expect an answer.
I am merely a dinosaur from television's Jurassic age.

However, I am most impressed, Madam President,
by your glossy brochure for this term.
It is lavishly yet tastefully illustrated,
like *Hello!* magazine, with a large and glamorous photograph of *you*,
and a small and hideous photo of *me*.
It is a public relations triumph
worthy of Peter Mandelson and Max Clifford.

We had nothing like this at the turn of the half-century,
and nothing like the bizarre event
which I see advertised for tomorrow night here:
Peter Stringfellow, described as "London's most infamous playboy",
is coming here "to teach students how to have fun".
I don't want to sound intolerant.
But anyone who has to be taught
how to have fun by Peter Stringfellow
is in an advanced state of clinical depression.

What is the world coming to? Tomorrow night Peter Stringfellow.
Tonight Jeffrey Archer. Who next?

In the golden age, Madam President, this old place
was purely and simply for debating, reading and drinking,
all of which we did with relentless application.

Which brings me to this important motion.
I now realise why you have invited *me*.
Because I am an expert in failure.
I failed at the Bar. I failed in Politics. I failed in Television.
I am a *serial* failure.

At the Bar my contemporaries (such as the ex-President from Balliol,
the noble Lord, Lord Mayhew)
went on to win the glittering prizes.
I, alas, fell by the wayside
and sank into the obscurity of the television studios.

In politics, I look back to 1959.
That was a year of great electoral significance.
A defining moment in the 20th century.
1959 was the year Margaret Thatcher succeeded in entering Parliament.
1959 was also the year
in which I *failed* to enter Parliament.
Such are the quirks of the popular will
by which the destiny of great nations is decided.

In fact, I have failed in everything –
I have even failed to become a member of the House of Lords.
Almost anyone seems to get in there nowadays!

To measure my failure in television,
I only have to look at those who have achieved success
as the dazzling *stars* of the medium – Frost, Paxman, Parkinson.
Why them and not me?

Of course, the BBC never understood me.
They would never let me have an orchestra.
A small band would have been enough,
so that I could dance down the studio steps
to conduct a rousing discussion
on Bovine Spongiform Encephalopathy.

When I last spoke at a debate here in 1967,
the motion was in Latin: *Quales artifices perimus,*
a well-known soundbite from Suetonius
which I need not translate for you, Madam President.

Nothing so scholarly tonight – *this* motion is simply an epigram,
but by whom, you may wonder.
Dr Johnson, of course? No. He wrote:
"Patriotism is the last refuge of the scoundrel."

Who borrowed that and cynically rewrote it
into the epigram we have here?
None other than our old friend Oscar Wilde.
It is, of course, one of his notorious
Phrases & Philosophies for the Use of the Young.
These were contributed by Wilde in 1894
to an undergraduate magazine in Oxford called *Chameleon,*
about the contents of which
he was to be fiercely cross-examined at the Old Bailey.

But not even the Marquis of Queensberry's counsel
could find anything perverted
in this innocent epigram about ambition and failure.
So I can happily commend this motion
as a message from the Master for the use of the young.

According to a kind viewer, who writes regularly to me,
I have now "reached the departure lounge of life".
My only ambition is that my plane can be delayed

so that I can attend the historic banquet
in this hall on April 17th.
That's when the Union's first eleven will be playing –
Heath, Heseltine, Hague, and Chancellor Jenkins –
a feast of oratory from the Society's immortals
which I shall enjoy, albeit in silence,
with even more than my usual humility.

I beg to support this motion.

TO THE LAST OF THE TOFFS

41

April 19th, 1998, at the Garrick Club's annual dinner. My speech was to propose the health of the Guest of Honour, who was my old friend Paddy Mayhew. He is more properly called Lord Mayhew of Twysden, QC, formerly Sir Patrick Mayhew, Secretary of State for Northern Ireland in John Major's Cabinet.

This dinner happened to be held just a week after the "Good Friday agreement" on Ulster's future. Thus in proposing Paddy's health I was conscious of his part as Secretary of State in helping to start the so-called "peace process". But anything more than a brief reference to this would not have been appropriate at this very non-political dinner.

There were one or two aspects of his career I was able to point out which have not normally been mentioned. The adjective most often attached to his name in the press has been "patrician", perhaps because of his voice, his height or his manner. But Paddy has never been the least bit patrician to me.

The other day, Mr Chairman, I was happily sitting under the stairs,
having drawn the winning horse
in the Club Grand National sweepstake,
when I was kindly awakened
by one of our most authoritative
and sophisticated members:

I see you're proposing the toast to Mayhew
at the annual dinner. So you won't have to say very much.
Because there's only one thing to be said about Paddy:
he's "the last of the toffs".
That's what he is.
That's all you need to say,
'The last of the toffs'."

So, Mr Chairman, that would appear to be that.
However, I have decided, reluctantly, to add a word. Or two.

Yet in searching for anything else to say,
I have regrettably been unable to discover anything to his discredit –
not even from former Cabinet colleagues.

It is nearly half a century since our paths first crossed.
That was when we were undergraduates.
One of my functions then was to write a review of debates
with critical impressions of promising newcomers.

To take a name at random, but with relish,
there was a Mr William Rees-Mogg, aged 21.
I delicately reported that he had made a "thoughtful speech
which improved as it proceeded".
Which was just as well, I can tell you.

I also noted another promising fellow, a Mr Patrick Mayhew,
aged 20, who "rolled out picturesque metaphors
in an impressive voice".
Which he has gone on doing ever since.

Two or three years later, I was a pupil barrister
appearing in a *cause célèbre*
at the Sevenoaks magistrates' court.
It was a case of driving without due care, or something.
To my pleasant surprise, there, sitting in the public seats,
was young Paddy Mayhew,
then still a Bar student, who had come to watch justice in action.

He gave me lunch in his nearby stately home,
and I happily gave the future Attorney General
some invaluable advice,
from my own virtually non-existent professional experience.

Paddy, of course, went on to win
the glittering prizes of his profession.
I, alas, fell by the wayside, and disappeared
into the obscurity of the mass media.

About 25 years later, in 1979, we met again.
He had taken silk, entered Parliament
and become a Minister whom I had to interview
on bended knee, with all the humility at my command.

His first ministerial job was Parliamentary Under-Secretary of State
at the Department of Employment.
He had been put there by Margaret Thatcher.
She told his ministerial boss, Jim Prior, "I am determined
to have *someone* with backbone in your Department."

Then, for the next 18 years, Paddy Mayhew
was continually in ministerial office.
Others rose and fell, Paddy rose and rose.
He stayed put in one job after another.
This led one of his more disposable Cabinet colleagues
to accuse him of having a "prehensile bottom".

Our Guest of Honour is a unique figure in several ways.
He is the only barrister MP
who never wanted to be a Law Officer.
He is the only Law Officer
who never wanted to be Lord Chancellor.
And he is the only politician whose one ambition
was to be Secretary of State for Northern Ireland –
which some politicians would see *not* as promotion but as punishment.

But Paddy was not deterred by Anglo-Irish history,
in which he is steeped, nor even discouraged
by the legendary words of Churchill
long ago in 1922:

"Great empires ..." said Churchill
(he was orating about the colossal upheaval of World War I),
"great empires have been overturned.
The whole map of Europe has been violently altered ...
all have encountered tremendous changes
in the deluge of the world,
but as the deluge subsides and the waters fall short,
we see the dreary steeples
of Fermanagh and Tyrone emerging once again.

The integrity of their quarrel,"
said Churchill, "is one of the few institutions
that has been unaltered in the cataclysm
which has swept the world."

Mr Chairman, Paddy Mayhew was under no illusions
when he took on Northern Ireland.
He had strong family reasons for wanting the job.
And, incidentally, Paddy's appointment to the Cabinet
in that capacity must have given the PM
special satisfaction for a personal reason:
the Prime Minister remembered that when Paddy was Minister of State
at the Home Office back in 1981,
he appointed as his Parliamentary Private Secretary,
as his Westminster dogsbody,
a young unknown called John Major.

It was Paddy who gave John Major his first leg up the greasy pole.
A brilliant flash, you may think,
of uncanny foresight on Paddy's part?
But Paddy makes no such extravagant claim.
He told Mr Major's biographer,
"John was everything a PPS ought to be,
but not an obvious future Prime Minister."

But, Mr Chairman, when we think about it,
were *any* Prime Ministers, when in their 30s,
obviously destined for No. 10? Not even Churchill?
No, the young Winston was hugely mistrusted
and was written off by many
as "a genius without judgement".

Thatcher? What was she 25 years ago?
A future Prime Minister? No, she was Heath's statutory woman.
Tony Blair? What was he ten years ago?
William Hague? What is he now?

But I have wandered slightly from my theme.
In his four years as Solicitor-General,
followed by five years as Attorney,
Paddy Mayhew was no run-of-the-mill Law Officer.

He was one of the most highly respected
Law Officers of recent years.

He must be one of the very few Solicitors-General
to have delivered an opinion
which led almost to the disintegration of a Cabinet,
and nearly to the fall of a Prime Minister.
The confidential opinion he delivered as Solicitor-General,
which warned Michael Heseltine of "material inaccuracies"
in his presentation of the Westland Helicopter case,
was leaked by Downing Street.
The Solicitor-General was not pleased.
On her way to the emergency debate, Margaret Thatcher said
to someone in Downing Street, "I may not be PM by 6.00 tonight."

This is not a legal occasion, nor is it a political occasion.
But may I just say this?
If, and it is still a big if, there is now going to be
a lasting peaceful settlement
of the Irish quarrel,
much credit, very much credit,
will be due to the determination, patience and courage
of Paddy Mayhew.

We, his friends and fellow Garrick members,
have understood that in his five difficult
and dangerous years in Northern Ireland,
he could not be among us here
as often as he would have liked.

These lines by Kingsley Amis were surely written
for Paddy Mayhew whenever he managed to arrive here
just in time for dinner, after a hellish day in Belfast:

> When pressures of the world become intense
> And humankind seems destitute of sense,
> With none but fools and madmen everywhere,
> Come to the Garrick for relief from care.

I can reveal that, after law and politics,
he is now pursuing another interest.

He is writing the life of his great-grandfather,
the Victorian statesman Viscount Goschen.
George Goschen became Chancellor of the Exchequer –
to everyone's surprise and to his own –
when Lord Randolph Churchill resigned in 1886.
This earned Goschen his place in history
as "the man whom Randolph Churchill forgot".

So with a great-grandfather who was a Viscount,
Paddy is *more* than a toff, he's almost a grandee.
But the best judgement on him that I have seen was this:
"Patrick Barnabas Burke Mayhew …"
(I forgot to mention that he is also descended from Edmund Burke!)
"Patrick Barnabas Burke Mayhew is a gentleman to his bootstraps."

I give you the toast – Paddy Mayhew.

MILTON SHULMAN 42

M ay 13th, 1998. A speech as Chairman of Foyle's Literary Luncheon at the Grosvenor House Hotel in honour of Milton Shulman's memoirs, *Marilyn, Hitler & Me.*

This was a long-awaited pleasure. For several years I had heard Milton Shulman's riveting stories about his life. I kept saying, "Don't tell *me*, write it in your memoirs."

When, after about 50 years on the *Evening Standard*, he was fired, and no longer had a column, he wrote his memoirs at last. Of course, he had much material all ready to draw on and my "encouragement" was merely irrelevant banter.

Milton Shulman has been one of the great media characters of post-war London. He has moved in many circles, theatreland, Fleet Street, television. But his greatest pride and joy is in his gifted and glamorous family, who were all at this Foyle's Luncheon. Before my speech I introduced them all:

His wife, Drusilla Beyfus, whom Milton extols for her "beauty, vivacity and talent".

Alexandra Shulman, his elder daughter, who is Editor of *Vogue*.

Nicola Shulman, his younger daughter, a journalist, who is Marchioness of Normanby and has made Milton, the Canadian son of a Ukrainian immigrant, the grandfather of an Earl, which delights him not a little.

And Jason Shulman, his son, a magazine art director and designer. When I sat down Milton, aged 80, more or less, rose to talk about his memoirs, about Marilyn, about Marlene, about Beaverbrook, about Martin Bormann and, of course, about Mr Goldberg.

Miss Foyle, Ladies and Gentlemen:

I feel even more unqualified for my job here today
than Milton Shulman felt just 50 years ago,
when Lord Beaverbrook offered him
the job of film critic.
The conversation in Arlington House was short:

"Mr Shulman, what do ye know about films?"
 Not very much.
"Do ye go to films?"
 Not very often. About once a month.
"Good. Just the man we want: a fresh mind on films."

Now, why am *I* here? Who, after all, am I?
That is a rhetorical question which does not call for an answer.
But I will tell you. I am merely an old friend –
someone who can be relied on for gross flattery on this occasion.

In November 1950, Miss Christina Foyle
was holding the 223rd of her famous Literary Luncheons
here in this very hotel.
It was the age of austerity and food rationing.
The book being honoured was much better
than the lunch being eaten.

The book was called *How to be a Celebrity*.
It was a collection of interview-profiles
of any personalities who then mattered.
The author was a handsome young Canadian journalist
who had himself begun to matter.

Here we are today at the 654th Foyle's Literary Luncheon,
this time for the memoirs of a somewhat older
and, he thinks, an even more handsome Canadian journalist.

What a multifarious, multi-faceted life he has led.
Originally in Toronto he studied to be a lawyer.
He then became a crooner – briefly.
He was then known, for the first
and the last time in his life, as "Whispering Milt".

Only considerations of time now restrain me
from rendering some of his repertoire as a crooner in 1934:
"It's Only a Shanty in Old Shanty Town",
"Sweet Sue"
and "The Sheik of Araby".
I can hear it now. Perhaps, later, Milton will oblige.

Look at what he went on to become:
barrister, wartime tank officer, secret intelligence officer,
war historian – whose work is still a classic –
Fleet Street reporter, film critic, drama critic,
book reviewer, television producer,
novelist, author of ten books (now 11)
and radio broadcaster,
who Stopped the Week for 18 years.
And, not least, winner of the prestigious Goldberg Award,
given to himself, by himself,
for telling vintage Jewish jokes,
of which there is one,
and sometimes two, on almost every page.

It is all in here. How the Canadian son of a Ukrainian immigrant
went to war against Hitler
and went to work for Lord Beaverbrook.
How this man's torrential outpouring of words and opinions
made him one of the biggest noises
in the cultural life of England's capital city for half a century.

No one who has lived here has not at one time or another
been instructed, illuminated, informed, infuriated
and probably insulted by Milton Shulman.

This book is the story of his turbulent career as a critic,
but there are also personal revelations and confessions
about himself, women, marriage, money, television, art,
sex, politics – everything.

About why he eventually abandoned
the far left-wing socialism of his youth.
He realised, rather late in life,
that true freedom was incompatible
with any form of Marxism.
Or it may have been that he did not wish
to be the only Marxist resident in Eaton Square!

And don't expect your usual run-of-the-mill book of memoirs,
which begin at the beginning
and keep right on to the end sequentially.

Oh, no! This is a magnificent, rumbustious hotch-potch,
switching back and forth from anecdote to opinion.

Many a famous name is dropped,
from Marlene Dietrich to Marilyn Monroe,
from Field-Marshal von Rundstedt to Martin Bormann,
from Kenneth Tynan to Robert Robinson.
Oh, yes! All human life is here!
Bewildered you may be, but you will not be bored.

As to Marilyn Monroe: Milton spent six weeks with her.
What was their relationship?
I have made a close analysis of the textual evidence.
He confesses that he was "starstruck"
and "hypnotised" by "close proximity" on a sofa
"to America's most enticing sex object".
But he then claims that his "only reaction
to the proximity of that 'enticing sex object'
was a paternal desire to pat her on the head".
A "paternal desire"? "To pat her *on the head*"?
Members of the jury, it is a matter for you.

With great eloquence and power,
he spells out the principles and philosophy
which guided him as a theatre critic.
He defends the campaigns he has fought,
often alone, notably against television
for encouraging violence among the young.

For all his many hobby-horses –
his books, his broadcasting, his campaigns –
first and foremost he has been a newspaper man,
one who writes five or six hundred
forceful and readable words
to meet a demanding deadline at dawn or midnight.

If Rudyard Kipling had known Milton Shulman,
he would surely have written these lines of him:

He hath sold his heart
To that old black art
We call the daily press.

That, incidentally, was a favourite quotation of Lord Beaverbrook,
Milton's mentor, and Fleet Street's greatest mischief-maker.
And never did Lord Beaverbrook make more or better mischief
than when he appointed young Milton Shulman
as his film critic – except, of course,
when he appointed young Milton Shulman as his theatre critic.

Ladies and Gentlemen, in the history of the *Evening Standard*
the name of Milton Shulman
ranks with that newspaper's most brilliant contributors –
David Low, Michael Foot, Randolph Churchill
and Charles Wintour, Editor for over 20 years.

Milton generously says in his acknowledgement
that I encouraged him
in the writing of these memoirs.
Very kind of him but quite ridiculous.
Does anyone seriously imagine
that Milton Shulman needed encouragement
to blow his own trumpet for 400 pages?

No. All that happened was that after a heated argument over lunch,
when his years as a columnist had come to an end,
I said to Milton:

Milton! Thou should'st be writing at this hour.
England hath need of thee.
She is a fen of stagnant waters.

But that's quite enough of Wordsworth, and of me.

43 MY 50TH

October 24th, 1973, St James's Gardens, Holland Park, at a dinner party for my 50th birthday at home. This little speech comes here at the end, out of chronological order, because I did not intend to include it. It is very personal. But I decided to add it to this collection because it was a wonderful private evening, beautifully organised by my then wife, Katherine, who was pregnant at the time. And because my gentle insults were tolerantly received by those at whom they were aimed.

Our guests were Lord and Lady Chalfont, Sir Geoffrey and Lady Cox, Ronald and Sarah Waterhouse, Dick and Janice Taverne, Godfrey and Mary Smith, Roderick and Emily MacFarquhar, Peter and Mary Cooper, John and Sally Thompson, George and Pam Ffitch, Peter and Jennifer Blaker, Ivan Yates, Kristin Shay, and Kenneth Bradshaw.

Some weeks later, I suffered an early experience of feminist extremism, which was then beginning to catch on. An article about me quoted one of the wives at this party (I never did discover who it was) as saying, "Robin referred in his speech only to the husbands and not to the wives." This was true, but it was *not* true to suggest that therefore I was a male chauvinist. My speech referred only to each man simply because I did not know all the wives well enough to pay them personal compliments, let alone make jokes at their expense. Either I had to drop all jokes about the husbands, which would have meant a jokeless speech, or to make no jokes about the wives. I took the latter course. At the time, nobody seemed to mind.

My Lord, Ladies and Gentlemen:

I must begin by pointing out an indisputable fact,
that since my 40th birthday,
which many of you helped to celebrate,
ten long years have elapsed.

For some of us, as Harold Macmillan says,
the autumn leaves are beginning to turn.
As a group are we not, in this permissive age,
a shining example of fidelity and constancy?
The same old husbands with the same old wives.

What I really meant to say was that
all our wives look ten years younger,
which, as a male chauvinist pig would say,
is a great tribute to their husbands.

As to the men, the ravages of time have taken their toll.
For all of you, the last ten years have been a restless decade
of change and challenge, of success and failure.
You have indulged your vaulting ambition,
and your insatiable lust for power.

Except for two of you, whose lifestyle
has remained simple and solitary,
uncorrupted by worldly desires,
untouched by ephemeral trends:
I refer to Ivan[1] and Kenneth.[2]

Ivan has steadfastly upheld
his sovereign independent status,
though his name has been increasingly linked
with that of Miss ——.
Ivan continues to be greatly valued
on the *Observer* as Fleet Street's greatest authority
on obscure bishops and eccentric headmasters.

---

[1] Ivan Yates of the *Observer* sadly died two years after this dinner party (see Speech 6).

[2] Kenneth Bradshaw, a senior House of Commons clerk, later the Clerk of the House.

What of Kenneth? The confidential clerk
who remains married to the entire House of Commons.
His classic work of scholarship,
Parliament and Congress, has sold more copies
than any other book on the subject –
it being the only one.

For the rest of you, these ten years
have been a decade of ruthless self-advancement,
an endless quest for those glittering prizes.

Ronald,[1] for instance,
who proposed my health so eloquently.
He has taken silk, after building up
what his obituary will one day describe
as a flourishing practice in the
remote hills of North Wales.

Alun Chalfont[2] has taken ermine,
the warmer thereby to maintain his socialist faith.

Geoffrey Cox[3] too has become a man of title.
He has received one of the more deserving knighthoods
of the last administration
for services which cannot be fully revealed.
He is now printing money in Newcastle
as Chairman of Tyne Tees Television.

John Thompson[4] now hands out licences
to print money in commercial radio,
being sternly disloyal to his friends in the process.
If there is a Queen's Award for Mobility of Labour,
John deserves it. He has been through more jobs
than any of us for the last ten years.

[1] Ronald Waterhouse, QC, later High Court judge for 18 years.

[2] Lord Chalfont later became a life peer on joining Harold Wilson's 1964 Government.

[3] Sir Geoffrey Cox was knighted as the founding Editor of *News at Ten.*

[4] John Thompson, CBE, formerly of the *Observer,* now worked for the Independent
Broadcasting Authority.

Some of us have broken long attachments
or have given up old haunts.
George Ffitch[1] has given up television to exercise his brain.
Dick Taverne[2] has given up Harold Wilson
and now belongs to a political movement
in whose leader he has the fullest confidence.

Rod MacFarquhar,[3] after holding himself out
for years as an expert Sinologist,
has actually been to China.
He has now emigrated to Belper
in the hope of becoming the new George Brown.

Peter Blaker,[4] who we were all certain
would rise to be a Parliamentary Under-Secretary,
has found his true destiny in the Commons
as the voice of Blackpool.
He resents any suggestion (not by me)
that Blackpool be offered
as the next nuclear testing site.

Peter Cooper's[5] career has been chequered.
He now works for the only human being
who actually looks like a Scotland Yard Identikit picture, David Frost.

Godfrey Smith[6] has pursued a policy of expansion.
He now owns five-and-a-half acres in Wiltshire.
He has come a long way since those far-off days in Oxford
when he had a lean and hungry look.

---

[1] George Ffitch, once of ITN, later Political Editor of *The Economist* and Managing Director of the London Broadcasting Company.

[2] Dick (now Lord) Taverne, QC, had left the Labour Party to be an Independent, thus the forerunner of the SDP.

[3] Roderick MacFarquhar, one-time *Panorama* colleague, founding Editor of the *China Quarterly*, later Labour MP for Belper, who is now a professor at Harvard.

[4] Peter Blaker (now the Rt Hon Lord Blaker, KCMG) was Tory MP for 18 years, and became Minister of State for Defence.

[5] Peter Cooper pursued a lively career in commerce.

[6] Godfrey Smith, novelist, anthologist and columnist, then, as now, on the *Sunday Times*.

As for myself, still in the same humble rut,
putting the same questions as ten years ago about inflation,
except that the percentages are higher.
I look forward to ending my TV career
in the way that George Ffitch has suggested,
by starting an interview with Harold Wilson
with, "What is the answer to my first question?"

I am very happy to have had your presence,
but nothing makes me happier than
Kathy's contribution to the population explosion.

This has been a beautiful way to celebrate a man's half-century.

POSTSCRIPT

W histler, the 19th-century artist and mordant wit, was asked, "For two days' labour you ask 200 guineas?" Whistler retorted, "No, I ask it for the knowledge of a lifetime."

The same principle applies to the relatively minor art of speech-making, of which I happen to have had some 60 years' experience. I started at school aged 15, making a speech, to my shame, in defence of the Munich Agreement. My speech-making has been as an amateur not as a professional. But a lifetime's experience has enabled me to practise the art, and to acquire the knack. So my value, if not in guineas, is knowledge acquired of speech-making in a lifetime of practice.

The speeches in this book have all been delivered on special, non-political, often unserious occasions – celebratory, commemorative or congratulatory. Such occasions are not insignificant in our public and social life.

Unfortunately, speeches made at these events tend to be dire and tasteless, without eloquence or elegance. Speech-making with style, wit and humour is nowadays a neglected art. It is out of keeping with prevailing prejudice against anything coherent, articulate, graceful or civilised. Do I exaggerate? I think not. Anyone who has attended a public dinner, or any similar function where speeches have to be made, will have noticed that the speech-making is often worse than the food.

Are there any techniques behind the art, any tricks of the trade, any advice to be offered to aspiring speech-makers? There are, of course, in every art, its unseen techniques and methods developed by the professional – how an actor acts, how a painter paints, how a speech is made. Such hidden techniques may be the subject of master-class instruction or teach-yourself manuals. This book is not such a thing. It is merely for entertainment, not for instruction. It is to be dipped into and savoured, not studied as

---

[1] My companion debater then is now the Rt Hon Sir Geoffrey Johnson Smith, MP.

part of a course for a speech diploma.

In American universities, as I discovered 50 years ago on an undergraduate debating tour,[1] they have degrees in speech, professors of speech, faculties of speech and coaches of debate. We had points awarded for logic, presentation, argumentation, humour and even gestures. One faculty member at the University of Illinois approached me and said, "Those gestures of yours were terrific. I made a careful note of them." Needless to say, I was quite unaware of having made any gestures, terrific or otherwise.

To be fair, the American belief in speech training has relevance to many professions – law, communications, media and so on. But it is not suited to speech-making as an art, an art with style, wit and humour. This cannot be taught, but only acquired through experience and practice. All speakers have their own style. Everyone's technique of preparation and delivery is different, and not suitable for others. In this book you may have noticed at least a dozen different kinds of speech, each calling for different techniques. No tricks of the trade apply to every kind of speech or to every speech-maker.

There are, of course, some elementary rules that apply to all speakers, famous or obscure, and to all occasions, grand or humble. I would have thought that those rules were much too obvious to mention. But I understand there are intelligent and sophisticated people who are petrified and paralysed by the prospect of having to make a speech, especially at a social event like a wedding or a birthday.

So at the risk of preaching platitudes, here are basic *don'ts*, which I have not always obeyed.

- Don't make a speech without taking trouble, without careful preparation.

- Don't drink any alcohol, except after your speech. Even a slight sip to give yourself courage will cause you to stumble.

- Don't be too long – never longer than ten minutes. With applause and laughter, that, anyway, will be 15 minutes.

- Don't use long sentences with subordinate clauses. (Brackets may be OK on paper, but they don't work in a speech.)

- Don't be flowery, but don't be afraid to use unusual or unfamiliar words, like "fructify" or "climacteric". The audience may be puzzled but also flattered, and your reputation will be enhanced.

- Don't mutter or mumble, as actors do when accepting awards.

- Don't begin your speech with predictable or hackneyed opening words.

- Don't insert irrelevant jokes which have no connection with your theme. They will sound forced and unfunny.

- Don't ever laugh when delivering a joke or being witty, if only because, if it falls flat, you can sail serenely on regardless.

- Don't deliver off-colour jokes, especially if ladies are present. If you wish to sail close to the wind, prepare very carefully and keep your nerve.

- Don't ever read your speech from big, floppy pieces of paper. Cards, 20 x 12cm (8 x 5in), are infinitely easier to hold if there is no podium, and much more unobtrusive.

Perhaps these will be helpful, "or," as a great newspaper editor used to add to a doubtful leading article, "perhaps not". Long ago, in the 1960s, I made a well-intentioned and high-principled mistake. Interviewing was then beginning to be regarded as an art. I published a code of principles and conduct for the guidance of television interviewers. In those prehistoric days I was one of the very few practitioners. I felt I had a right and duty to publish my ten-point code. But as the Hammurabi of television's Jurassic Age, I had no lasting influence or effect whatever. Every point in my code has been violated every day since. This is not surprising. I had no Napoleonic authority as director of, or editor-in-chief of, anything. My authority was only that of an enthusiastic but lowly practitioner speaking to his peers.

Along with my code, I pontificated about interviewing technique and methods of preparation, all from my own experience which therefore did not apply to anyone else. It was all about how to do it, which really meant how *I* did it and wasn't necessarily how anyone else should do it.

Like interviewing or writing, speaking is an art or an aptitude which must depend on experience. That experience is personal and unique. It cannot be communicated to others except by the result, by hearing a speech, watching an interview or reading an article.

At a painter's exhibition, the pictures are displayed for enjoyment and scrutiny without explanation of how the painter's art is accomplished. So it is with the art of speech-making.

I hope, dear reader, that you have treated this book like a box of assorted delights – some sweet, some soft, some hard – from which you are welcome to take your pick. But please don't ask how to do it. Speaking for myself, even after a lifetime longer than Whistler's, I do not really know.

INDEX

[Names are given here as they were referred to, often informally, by Sir Robin as he spoke. So if these index references lack up-to-date styles or titles, this is not due to ignorance or discourtesy.]